∞

How to Love
as Jesus Loves

Francis P. Donnelly, S.J.

How to Love
as Jesus Loves

Unlocking the Treasures
of Christ's Sacred Heart

SOPHIA INSTITUTE PRESS®
Manchester, New Hampshire

How to Love as Jesus Loves: Unlocking the Treasures of Christ's Sacred Heart was originally published in 1911 by the Apostleship of Prayer, New York, under the title *The Heart of the Gospel: Traits of the Sacred Heart*. This 1999 edition by Sophia Institute Press includes editorial revisions to the original text and omits the preface and final chapter of the original edition.

Sophia Institute Press®
Box 5284, Manchester, NH 03108
1-800-888-9344
www.sophiainstitute.com

Imprimi potest: Joseph F. Hanselman, S.J., *Praepositus Prov.*,
Maryland/New York
Nihil obstat: Remigius Lafort, S.T.L., *Censor Deputatus*
Imprimatur: John M. Farley, Archbishop of New York
May 1, 1911

Library of Congress Cataloging-in-Publication Data

Donnelly, Francis P., 1869-
[Heart of the Gospel]
How to love as Jesus loves : unlocking the treasures of
Christ's sacred heart / Francis P. Donnelly.
p.   cm.
Originally published: The Heart of the Gospel.   New York :
Apostleship of Prayer, 1911.
ISBN 0-918477-99-9 (pbk. : alk. paper)
1. Sacred Heart, Devotion to.   I. Title.
BX2157.D63   1999
232 — dc21   99-23355   CIP

99 00 01 02 03 04 05 9 8 7 6 5 4 3 2 1

∞

To my father

Editor's note: The biblical references in the following pages are based on the Douay-Rheims edition of the Old and New Testaments. Where applicable, quotations from the Douay-Rheims edition have been cross-referenced with the differing numeration in the Revised Standard Version, using the following symbol: (RSV =).

∞

Contents

Christ's Sacred Heart is the perfect symbol of His love

"You are my friends, if you do the things I command you."

John 15:14

∞

Devotion is not to be identified with devotional practices any more than patriotism is with fireworks. A man may spend the great holidays quietly in his home, may saw wood on Washington's Birthday, and may read a book on the Fourth of July, but if he observes the laws of his country and practices the Ten Commandments, he will be a true patriot and he need not worry because he has not shouted himself hoarse hurrahing for the blessings of freedom, or burned his fingers setting off firecrackers, or even tired the muscles of his arm waving the Stars and Stripes. All of these actions are laudable and have their good effects. They are manifestations of patriotism, although not the highest manifestations, and they are means — and in some cases, necessary means — to enkindle and foster true patriotism.

Devotional practices are indeed much more necessary to devotion than all the usual means of displaying and stimulating patriotism are for the proper development of that virtue, yet a devotion may exist and be intense without having any particular and exceptional ways of manifesting itself. The hymns, the lights, the pictures, the beautiful shrines, the special services on certain days: these and many other excellent practices are required to arouse and keep alive true devotion. Without all that, there may often be reason to suspect the absence of devotion or to be skeptical of its intensity. By such displays, too, true devotion is exercised and developed, not wasting itself by use, but growing stronger, like a muscle, with exercise.

Devotional practices, then, are helpful and even necessary, but they do not constitute devotion. Light and air are helpful and necessary for life, but they are from without and life is from within, and devotion, too, is from within.

We sometimes hear good men say, "This business of devotion is not for me. I am not much for feeling or sentiment." What should be said in answer? These good people should be politely but firmly assured that they do not know what devotion is.

If devotion is not the same as devotional practices, neither is it the same as sentiment and feeling. True devotion is not feeling; it is willing. It is conviction, not sentiment. Feeling and sentiment are not always within our complete power. They may vary with the weather or with the pulse. Devotion does not watch the thermometer or fluctuate with the barometer. It does not disappear with our appetite and return after a good meal. Devotion belongs to the will and has its source in solid convictions. Give a man a firm, unyielding grasp of a truth; follow that up with a relentless determination to abide by that truth, and you have equipped a man with a full-fledged devotion.

Every year, many of our gallant firemen meet the death of heroes. Do they wait, when the alarm comes, for a gush of sweet feeling or the spur of sentiment to rouse them from sleep and put them in motion? They have no time to wait for such superfluities. As they rush to their post, hastily tightening their belts, one idea is uppermost in their minds: "There is a fire somewhere, and our place is to be there to put it out." That is their conviction; that is their willing. The next morning, perhaps, they may feel the warmth of feeling and sentiment, if they can find in the papers, as often they will not, the scanty recognition of their bravery. Do they have devotion? The noble deaths of so many are a testimony beyond the power of words to show that men who may not know how to define *devotion* or call it by its right name know well how to practice it in its highest and most unselfish form.

Yet, even if devotion is not perfect or perfected without some devotional practices, we may not deny the splendid influence of true feeling and right sentiment upon devotion. The man who would banish sentiment and feeling from the hearts of the world is an active worker for the return of the glacial period of very hard rock and very cold ice. Who would eclipse the dawning hopes of youth or draw the curtain of twilight over the sunset memories of old age? Must all the canvas on which are painted the pictures of the world be made into flour sacks, and all our monuments broken up to macadamize our roads? The eloquent vender of food tablets may prove by facts and figures, by analytical tables and accurate weights, that his vest-pocket breakfast has all the nutriment of a table d'hôte dinner, but the world will not be won away from its varied and substantial meal to any tasteless, odorless, colorless, sizeless substitute for a bill of fare.

If man were a machine, sentiment would be as useful as a bouquet on a locomotive. If we were all angels and had minds not continually swayed by conflicting currents of the body or forever unsettled by brilliant pictures of the imagination, then a truth would mean a resolution, and a resolution would mean an act, and we would leap without pause from duty to devotion. But we are not bodiless angels. We throb with feeling; we glow with sentiment.

Devotion is indeed conviction and willing, but true feeling and right sentiment must grace the path of duty, making conviction easier and willing prompter. Devotion will never produce its fullest and richest harvests unless feeling softens the soul and sentiments keep it ever warm. It is the purpose of many devotional practices — of pictures and songs and prayer meetings — to awaken these emotions, to stir up the soul to some of its untouched depths, and so to elicit the full cooperation of soul and body in realizing all the results of devotion.

∞

The devotions of the Church have all enriched her, but none perhaps more so than devotion to Christ's Sacred Heart.

Devotion to Christ's Sacred Heart is devotion to the love of Christ. It comes from a profound conviction that Christ is our true friend, that at first He was God without a human nature and that afterward He became man — became Christ — all for us and to show His friendship for us. "God so loved the world as to give His only-begotten Son."[1] Christ our Lord was born of friendship for us, had no other reason for every breath of life He drew except friendship for us, and did not hesitate to give the supreme test of the most loving friendship by going to His death for us.

[1] John 3:16.

The fireman says, "My conviction is that I should be at the fire; my determination is to get there as soon as possible." He is devoted to his duty. Let any man say, "My conviction is that Christ was and is my friend; my determination is to show myself His friend," and he is devoted to the Heart of Christ and will be ready with the brave fireman to make sacrifices — and heroic ones — if his duty calls for them.

But why, it may be asked, do we speak of devotion to the Sacred Heart instead of devotion to Christ? The question may be answered by another. Why do nations have flags? Why do causes have their rallying cries, and colleges their colors and cheers? Why do we speak of the Wars of the Roses? Why of the thistle of Scotland and the shamrock of Ireland? Why else but because we want a brief, telling way of summing up and expressing what we hold most dear? A word will do service for a thought, will hold it and keep it for centuries still fresh and green. So a symbol will express a whole cause, explain it, and enshrine it forever.

Symbols many and various have been seen among men, but where has there been one more touching, more significant, than the heart? The Heart of Christ is the symbol, the representation, the expressive picture of the love of Christ. Every language has made the heart a synonym for love, and the Heart of Christ signifies Christ's love and bears in all its details the strongest and most lasting proofs of that love.

Whether devotion to the Heart of Christ inspires new deeds or vivifies with new meaning the customary actions of a man's life, it will put a purpose into them that was not there before. His heart will go out to his friend, his benefactor, his crucified Savior; it will flame with the motives of gratitude, love, and reparation. He will live his life influenced by such consoling convictions. He will be practicing true devotion to Christ's Sacred Heart, from which he will be learning to love as Jesus loves.

∞

*How to Love
as Jesus Loves*

Chapter One

∞

Christ intercedes for you

"Mary kept all these words,
pondering them in her heart."

Luke 2:19

∞

"Putting two and two together" is a simple expression for a sublime and fruitful work. Man and man alone can put two and two together. In that operation, man is severed from the beasts by a chasm which only God's omnipotence can bridge, because to put two and two together is the operation of a spiritual soul. By the same operation, man gains experience, science, and wisdom. Now, it is that same simple, yet sublime work that goes on in the heart of prayer — the same that went on in its perfect form in the most perfect heart of prayer among men. St. Luke, describing the events of our Lord's birth and, recounting the story told by the shepherds of the angels' apparition, says that "Mary kept all these words, pondering them in her heart." "Pondering them in her heart" means, in the Latin and the Greek, what we may describe by the homely phrase "putting two and two together."

What must a man do to put two and two together? He must understand clearly; he must deliberate; he must affirm or deny that the single twos belong together; and he must draw a conclusion. By reflecting then on what he has done, he may draw far-reaching principles, and, associating other similar conclusions, he may draw other principles. Principles are then put together, and order arises; and from order, system and science and then wisdom. Such are the fruits of "pondering" over the treasures of the heart, fruits that Mary gathered in their full-ness and richest ripeness.

Take a similar but far inferior case. St. Ignatius of Loyola[2] spent nine months in the cave of Manresa, pondering the truths of God, weighing them, ordering them, and combining them. The results of that season of prayer we still have in the consummate science and wisdom of his *Spiritual Exercises*.

Oh, if only we had the wisdom that grew and filled Mary's heart, from her lifetime of pondering, from her Immaculate Conception to the Annunciation, from the Annunciation to the Ascension, from the Ascension to her Assumption! The volume of that prayerful heart would contain all the revealed truth which St. John declared all the books of the world could not hold,[3] and it would contain much more, because the trea-sures of Mary's heart were more numerous and more precious and more perfectly pondered than the riches of St. John. St. Thomas Aquinas[4] put all theology into an epitome called the *Summa Theologica*. Mary's heart of prayer was the epitome of all God's dealings with man — is it too daring to say? — God's *Summa*.

How, then, shall we describe Mary's heart of prayer when it took to pondering the Heart of Christ? Jesus was her all, her universe, and His Heart was that universe's central sun, surely not separated in her loving and prayerful pondering from the effulgence of the divinity which invested that Heart and

---

[2] St. Ignatius of Loyola (1491-1556), founder of the Society of Jesus.

[3] Cf. John 21:25.

[4] St. Thomas Aquinas (c. 1225-1274), Dominican philosopher and theologian.

which divinized the mother's perfect affection, transforming supreme love into supreme worship.

St. John heard once the beating of that Heart. He straightway became the "one whom Jesus loved,"[5] and his thoughts soared to distant heights and circled to far-off horizons, cognizant of visions hitherto beyond mortal ken. If nearness to the Heart of Christ was at least a partial cause of St. John's ecstasies (and who can doubt it?), what shall we say of the pondering of her whose heartbeat was once His heartbeat, who long enjoyed a mother's privilege and blessing, whose sensitive ear caught every echo, even the faintest, of joy or sorrow that sounded in her Son's Heart, and whose motherly love realized those emotions more fully, more deeply than any other could possibly do, "pondering them in her heart"?

∞

Christ, it is true, was known in prophecy, but it was Mary's heart that was the first to know Him in realization. There was nothing on Mary's side to dim or tarnish that knowledge. What was offered was received, undiminished and unblemished. When the Heart of Christ, therefore, in its turn, would take to pondering, where would it turn, prompted by every noble impulse, more surely than to the heart of Mary?

If a mirror is perfect, it gives back the image perfectly. No flaws or blurs on its polished surface impair the reflection. In fact, a perfect mirror is not seen at all; it is lost in its reflection. Such, no doubt, was the reflection of Christ in Mary's heart. There was no self there, no blurring, no impairing of the

---

[5] John 20:2.

knowledge and love of her Son as they radiated from her heart. Christ, then, would see in her one responding perfectly to His grace, and, from His pondering that fact, there would be an answering reflection from His Heart.

Then would arise the exquisite rivalry of loving hearts. Imagine, if you can, where it would end in the case of Jesus and Mary. Put two polished mirrors face-to-face and a lighted candle between them. Your eye will be bewildered with the multiplied views of the tiny flame, stretching away in the distance. The rays of light leap from surface to surface, giving rise to an endless succession of images. Perhaps that picture will help you to realize the depths and deepenings of love as Jesus and Mary pondered one another in their hearts with ever new interchanges and reproductions of the light of love.

If Mary's heart gathered up in its loving meditations an epitome of Christian truths, Jesus, with His pondering Heart, could find in Mary's heart the epitome of His life and mission, of His Incarnation. He could watch every drop of His Heart-blood finding response in Mary. When sin would have seized upon Mary's soul at its creation, His blood was there to interpose between the destined victim and its inherited doom, and Mary's soul came into existence immaculate. In her, this greatest mystery of Christ's grace, as well as all other mysteries, received their exemplification. About her He saw the Holy Trinity concerned in the Annunciation. Upon her consent, His own Incarnation was made to depend. No, Christ would not have to look beyond Mary and Mary's heart to find a picture in miniature of the wondrous dealings of God with man.

We know, however, that the Heart of Christ, in its hours of prayer, thought of other hearts too. Sinful hearts, as well as

Mary's sinless heart, came within the scope of His pondering. It is good for us that they did so! We need the prayers of that divine Heart. "In the days of His flesh, with a strong cry and tears, offering up prayers and supplications to Him that was able to save Him from death, He was heard for His reverence."[6] The burden of our sins drew the strong cry from His lips and wrung the tears from His eyes, but He was heard, as He is heard now, too.

His priesthood is everlasting. "Whereby He is able also to save forever them that come to God by Him, always living to make intercession for us."[7] The unbelief of Thomas was the occasion of showing us that Christ did not permit His wounds to be closed.[8] They are still open, and the most eloquent intercession comes from the wound of the Heart. Nor is that silent prayer the only one now offered for us in Heaven. The Heart of Christ still ponders our sins and Mary's sinlessness, still prays to God for us, and is still heard for His reverence.

[6] Heb. 5:7.
[7] Heb. 7:25.
[8] Cf. John 20:24-27.

Chapter Two

∞

Christ reveals the strength of meekness

"Learn of me, because I am meek
and humble of heart."

Matthew 11:29

The one who first said that "meekness is not weakness" was the author of much more than a good rhyme. Meekness is a virtue, and for that reason, it is an exhibition of strength. No one would consider trained muscles — graceful, vigorous, and untiring — evidence of passiveness or weakness of body. The athlete is our ideal of a strong man. Now, virtues are the trained muscles of the will, by the help of which man exercises his freedom energetically, perseveringly, at the proper time, and in the proper way. Meekness, then, is strength, if to throttle a lion is strength, if to hold one's place on the fighting line is strength.

All virtues keep to the golden mean. They travel in the middle of the road; they swerve not to the side of excess, nor slip to the side of defect. Meekness has a hard road to travel. It holds the curb upon anger, keeping it to the path. The touchiness of resentment, the tenacity of revenge, the cry of rage becoming a curse, the fierceness of wrath that vents itself in abuse or blows: meekness must rule and govern these in their incessant manifestations along the way of life.

In this work, meekness should have occasions enough to display its strength, and yet it has another task, not so laborious, not so frequent, but often necessary. There are times when righteous indignation is called for, when the voice must be raised in protest and when energetic resistance becomes a duty. Meekness, then, must put spurs to the laggard soul, in order that it may not weaken or fail in life's journey.

So, there is the hard task of meekness — to keep the currents of our irascible nature at the proper temperature, not permitting them to be chilled into inactivity or to boil over into fiery vapors, but retaining them in sparkling, refreshing vigor anywhere between freezing and boiling point. Or, to put it another way, meekness performs the duties of a good policeman toward our inclinations to anger. It will not allow them to loiter when they should move on or to break the law in any way, as rarely listless anger is more prone to do.

Have you ever considered why our Lord said, "Learn of me, because I am meek and humble of heart"? Some have thought that He wished only to teach us the two virtues of meekness and humility in this passage. Such an interpretation neglects the rest of the passage in which those words occur. Christ was opening a school in opposition to that of the Pharisees. He invited all to come to it. "Take up my yoke upon you and learn of me, because I am meek and humble of heart; and you shall find rest to your souls. For my yoke is sweet and my burden light."[9] Never had any school a more attractive advertisement: The teacher was "meek and humble of heart"; the pupils would find rest for their souls; the lesson was sweet and easy. Christ, then, in calling Himself meek of heart, was describing the teacher to us and showing His qualifications for the position.

No doubt the first lesson the pupils would learn would be that of meekness, which displayed itself in every word and

[9] Matt. 11:29-30.

motion of their friend and teacher, especially as the Pharisees who conducted the rival school did not have the meekness of Christ.

The pupils of Christ might shudder at the words *yoke* and *burden* if they forgot how their meek teacher would fit yoke and burden sweetly to their shoulders and necks, and how, by His hands, He would make them light. Yokes are made for two, and the other one, they would recall, is Christ.

Meekness is properly of the heart. It is the safety valve of anger; it keeps the hot blood of the heart at a normal temperature. Anger, according to St. Thomas, has six daughters. The smallness of the family may excite some surprise, but the great theologian, in his usual way, shows why they are six and where they keep themselves. Two reside in the heart — wrath and revenge. Three live on angry lips — the scream, which is a confused cry, the abuse, which attacks the neighbor, and blasphemy, which execrates God. The last of these unlovely daughters is blows, the latest-born of the children of anger. Meekness has to manage this unruly household and does so by keeping the heart under its strong sway.

To call the roll of anger's brood will help us to appreciate better the meekness of Christ's Heart. We know that on rare occasions, meekness fired His Heart with zeal, put a lash in His hand, and kindled righteous indignation upon His lips. But, more frequently, the meekness of Christ is displayed in patience and gentleness.

There could not be in Christ the sinful strife of passions, but there could be the holy rivalry of virtues. Christ had real feelings and real passions, although not sinful ones. How many times meekness and righteous indignation struggled for the control of Christ's Heart, and how rarely did the victory go to the latter!

St. Mark pictures that struggle for us on one occasion where Christ knew that the Pharisees had determined upon His ruin, and He forced them by their silence to admit His right to heal on the Sabbath. "Looking around about them," relates St. Mark, "with anger, being grieved for the blindness of their hearts, He saith to the man, 'Stretch forth thy hand.' "[10] That was one occasion out of a multitude where meekness did not allow anger to flame into rebuke, but melted anger into grief.

The Passion shows us meekness winning its greatest triumph in the Heart of Christ. Justice might have summoned legions of angels, but meekness said to Peter, "Put away thy sword."[11] That is the constant cry of meekness: "Put away thy sword." The silence of Christ in His Passion is another manifestation of His meekness. "When He was reviled, He did not revile; when He suffered, He threatened not."[12] The silence of Christ was not the outcome of a want of feeling. He felt every pain, every insult in its full strength. He felt the waves of just anger ever beating and raging, but ever stayed by the unyielding firmness of meekness.

Even in His innermost thoughts during the Passion we may behold His meekness. The frightfulness of the torments to come, the dark deluge of sin, the lavish generosity of His

[10] Mark 3:5.
[11] Cf. Matt. 26:52.
[12] 1 Pet. 2:23.

Redemption and its futility in many cases: these were so many motives for His will to complain and rebel, but meekness preferred the shame and won another triumph at the expense of Christ's Heart-blood. "Not my will but Thine be done,"[13] said meekness with bloody lips. From that dearly bought victory until the end, meekness was king in the Heart of Christ, and around the throne stood all the fair children of that virtue, as beautiful as the daughters of anger are ugly. These were silence under lash and cross, the look of longing for the one who denied Him, the kiss of peace for the traitor, the prayer of forgiveness for all, the hands fettered forever in the widest embrace of love, and the Heart shedding its treasures upon the world, giving blood for blows, giving life for death.

Teach me, Christ, because Thou art meek of heart!

---

[13] Matt. 26:39.

Chapter Three

∞

Christ emptied Himself
to give Himself
completely to you

"Learn of me, because I am meek
and humble of heart."

Matthew 11:29

∞

All virtues practice humility. They recognize deficiencies and defects. They bow in submission to the law. You have seen soldiers stand at attention on the firing line and face the enemy. If there was no submission to one higher up, if there was no enemy to face, the army would disintegrate into the scattered aimlessness of a picnic. Humility is the discipline of the army of virtues, keeping them ever at attention, ever facing the foe, ever ready for the command "Forward."

When Christ our Lord opened His school and issued His prospectus, He promised His pupils perpetual meekness on the part of the teacher. That single qualification would ensure a full school, if the applicants were only certain that the meekness would outlast the opening day or the first class. Christ foresaw the misgivings of the candidates, and He hastened to add to His first qualification a second and crowning one: "I am . . . humble of heart."

The meekness would last. It would always remember that it had a high standard above it and a host of good qualities to attain to, because the meekness always would be humble of heart.

Everyone, therefore, would troop into the school of Christ, welcomed with a glad, abiding smile, with no shadow of a punishing rod lurking in the background. Even the bruised reed would enter there and have its fragile and torn fibers not crushed to powder, but mended into wholeness again. And the smoking flax would come in full confidence that the gracious, condescending teacher would stoop even to its feeble lowliness, and with the breath of charity kindle its dull, faint spark into the glowing flame of life.[14]

Yes, humility is a daily virtue in the great classroom of Christ, and pride daily haunts the schools of the Pharisees. Humility stoops, but pride holds its head high, treading on insignificant straws and stamping out the impertinent smoke of smoldering weeds. Both have their yokes and burdens; but, whereas humility studies carefully the weak muscles and tender flesh, fitting all with gentle, loving fingers, pride haughtily casts its yoke upon its slaves and arrogantly orders them to drag their cheerless burdens. Humility says with kindly voice, "Friend, go up higher." Pride thunders at its shamefaced followers, "Give this other man place."[15] Humility and pride begin all their sentences in the same way, but they end them all in opposite ways. Pride cries out, "I am not as the rest of men; O God, I give thee thanks, I am not unjust." Humility whispers, "I am not as the rest of men; God, be merciful to me, a sinner."[16]

How well humility was taught in the school of Christ is evident from the object lesson He gave in that virtue. The Pharisees were the forbidding examples of pride. Far different was the model of humility. In a splendid exhibition of true

[14] Cf. Isa. 42:3.
[15] Luke 14:10, 9.
[16] Luke 18:11, 13.

teaching, meek and humble teaching, Christ introduced His standard of humility to His Apostles: the child.[17]

The child is too small to look down; he looks up to others. He is too young to know he has excellences. He is too healthy and active to pose before a mirror. To be proud, one must reflect and be self-conscious. Children do not know that they are virtuous, and if they did know, they could not remember it long enough to be proud.

A true teacher must ever be humble. He is forever coming down to another man's level. Judged by that standard, how humble is the Heart of Christ, which stooped from the highest heights of divinity to the level of our humanity! To have humility, it is not necessary that one should be capable of pride or sin. The Heart of Christ could not sin, could not have defects, and yet it had the truest humility, because with all truly humble hearts, it saw that its riches came from God. Without God, it would be nothing. Christ need not have felt the humiliation unless He chose to, but He did choose to and did feel it.

Consider the successive depths of humility to which the Second Person of the Blessed Trinity descended. The Heart of Christ is the flower of the most sublime humility, stooping from Heaven to earth, the subjection of the divine to the human, an act which St. Paul made his supreme effort to describe by the words "emptying Himself and taking the form of slave."[18] Even in that infinite plunge, there were deeper depths. Christ

[17] Matt. 18:1-4.
[18] Phil. 2:7.

need not have subjected Himself to the conditions of human birth: the nine months, the swaddling clothes, the nursing, the ills and helplessness of infancy, the growth in wisdom and age. Had Christ come in the fullness of manhood, He would have avoided all that; but would we have had the same realization of His humble Heart? The Heart of Bethlehem and of Nazareth was not more humble than that of His public life, but it seems so to us, because the littleness of infancy and childhood is more obvious to us.

Still deeper did Christ's humility go. He put Himself below men's whims and desires, men's ignorance and vices. He was perpetually renouncing Himself and perpetually consoling others. In a sense, He renewed at every moment the humility of the Incarnation. His humanity, had He so desired, could have been transfigured and glorified from the first; but He clouded His divinity under the ordinary exterior of the ordinary man. Tabor lifted for a moment the eclipse of His humility,[19] but His Heart enshrouded itself once more and every moment denied its assumed nature the manifestation of the splendor and loveliness and joy of Heaven.

Yet, other and deeper abysses of humility yawned before that Heart, and down them it descended. At the feet of Peter and Judas, beneath the scourge of the soldiery, under the crown of mockery, upon the Cross of shame, into the desolation of the malefactor's tomb — there the humble Heart brought His tortured human nature.

Surely, in the Passion, the Heart of Christ sounded the fathomless depths of humility. Ah, no! It created a void still

[19] Cf. Matt. 17:2; Mark 9:2-3; Luke 9:29.

more profound into which it lowered itself. In the Incarnation, Christ emptied Himself of His divinity to become a man; in the Eucharist, He emptied Himself of His humanity, it might be said, to become food and drink. The Heart that could stoop to the bruised reed has passed into the ground wheat and the crushed grape.

As the pupil watches his Master cast Himself down where depths descend upon depths, it will not be so hard for him to stoop from the level of manhood to the slightly lower level of childhood.

Jesus, humble of Heart, make me one of these, Thy little ones!

Chapter Four

Christ teaches you perfect contrition

"He hath sent me to heal
the contrite of heart."

Luke 4:18

∞

Sorrow for sin is consoling. But the fretting of soul that arises because we have not come up to our own expectations is not true sorrow for sin. Sorrow for sin arises from a conviction that we have not come up to God's expectations. Remorse is indeed painful, but remorse is merely the clamor of conscience scolding the soul for its failures; it may lead to sorrow for the past, or the rebuke may be silenced by new and repeated excesses.

But true sorrow for sin is consoling. Pride may chafe us, because we are not as good as we thought we were; right reason may torture us, because we have acted through passion and wrong reason. Sorrow for sin, however, is humble and is submissive and obedient to right reason. Penitence is the healing of the contrite in heart.

When Christ our Lord asserted at Nazareth His claim to be the Messiah, He said, "The Spirit of the Lord is upon me. He hath sent me to heal the contrite of heart."[20] These words of Isaiah, which our Lord applied to Himself, do not mean that He came to heal the hearts broken and saddened by sin only. "Contrite of heart" includes all broken hearts, although by far the larger number of those who feel the touch of His healing

[20] Luke 4:18; Isa. 61:1.

29

hand are the hearts broken by the weight of sin. The Messiah came to console the penitent.

But are not tears the desired accompaniment of sorrow, and are not they the outward sign of desolation? How, then, can sorrow for sin be consoling? The answer is that tears may exist without penitence, and penitence may exist without tears. The pressure exerted by sorrow for sin is not upon the lachrymal glands, but upon the heart. Agitation of soul may fling off a few tears, as a storm whips the sea into flying flakes of spray, but it calls for a power in the sky mightier than a wind to lift the whole sea landward in a surging tide; and the power of penitence is not to be measured by falling tears, but by the lifting of the heart in response to the grace of God.

Nor are all tears scalding. Who will believe that the tears of Mary Magdalene, which fell so fast upon the feet of Christ, were signs of desolation, and not proof of her abundant love,[21] gushing out with the fullness and refreshing softness of a "long day's raining"? The tears of penitence are rather the overflow of God's grace. As long as the heart clings to sin, refuses to relinquish the hold of unlawful passion, and looks with satisfaction upon the past, there a barrier to God's grace. Let the heart, however, turn from what it before chose, and undo, as far as it can, the past; let it turn to God with an apology — for contrition is an apology of the heart to God — and the barrier will be lifted, and God's grace will roll in with a cleansing flood, and the pent-up heart will find relief in tears. Mary Magdalene was in desolation, perhaps, as, dry-eyed, she faced the staring guests at the banquet. But she was in consolation

---

[21] Luke 7:38, 47.

when she gazed upon our Lord with tearful eyes. There is a rainbow of hope in every sky looked at through the shower of penitent tears.

∽

St. John Chrysostom[22] has said that sorrow for sin is the only healing sorrow. Tears cannot recall a friend, staunch blood, close a wound, open a grave, or cure any other pain or loss, but tears can heal sin. And why? It is because the Heart of Christ put the healing power there, because His love sweetened the bitterness of tears.

In the Garden of Olives, our Lord made an act of contrition for the sins of mankind. As we all sinned in Adam, we all repented in Christ. He was "made a curse for us."[23] "Him, who knew no sin, He hath made sin for us, that we might be made the justice of God in Him."[24] Yet, the act of contrition in Christ's Heart does not supply wholly for the act of each soul. The sinner himself must give up his own sin, but, having done so, everything else before and after that act of the sinner's will is the fruit of God's grace. It is grace that prompts the act, sustains and elevates it, and blesses its results in time and eternity. Our own freedom must save our souls, as our own food must give sustenance to our bodies, but Christ's love, with more than the completeness and wonder of a mother's love, prepares the food for our wills, which are made more helpless than infants by sin. We have but to cooperate with His grace.

---

[22] St. John Chrysostom (c. 347-407), Bishop of Constantinople.

[23] Gal. 3:13.

[24] 2 Cor. 5:21.

Consider the perfection of the contrition found in the Heart of Christ. He could not be touched with sin, but "He was reputed with sinners, and upon Him was laid the iniquity of us all."[25] And for all of us He made reparation and He sorrowed, including in His sorrow every quality found in our far weaker contrition.

Contrition should be interior, in the heart. "Rend your hearts, not your garments, and turn to the Lord your God."[26] The rending of the Heart of Christ is witnessed to by a thousand messengers who have hurried out by every way they could to tell us in a language that cannot lie — the language of blood — that the sorrow of sin is crushing His Heart. The rending of His Heart is eloquent in the words in which He voices His contrition: "Not my will, but Thine be done."[27] From the will — that is, from the heart — came that act of contrition.

Contrition must be supernatural. God must enter into the sorrow for sin. The Heart of Christ expressly excluded all thought of self, all motives that led away from God. Even the passing of the chalice that God's justice held to His lips was not to be effected by His will. God's will might remove it; Christ's will would not. So then, the draining of the chalice was accomplished with the purest unselfishness: "Not my will, but Thine be done."

Contrition should be sovereign. Never did a heart have to make more fearful reckoning between the worth of God and

---

[25] Cf. Isa. 53:12, 6.
[26] Joel 2:13.
[27] Matt. 26:39.

the price of sin than the Heart of Christ made, and never was the infinite value of God's law asserted more emphatically. On one hand was the whole Passion to come, with all its tortures of body and soul; on the other hand was God's justice. Christ accepted the sorrow, the suffering, the disgrace and death. He laid His Heart upon the altar of God's justice and was Himself the priest who completed the sovereign holocaust: "Not my will, but Thine be done."

Contrition must be universal. Was there a single sin exempted from God's will? Was there a single wish of God's will that was not embraced by the Heart of Christ? Was there a single pang of pain, a single twinge of sorrow, a single drop of His blood excluded from the generous offer of Christ? There can be only one answer to these questions. The "my" of Christ included all that the "Thy" of the will He addressed included: "Not my will, but Thine be done."

It is, then, that great act of contrition which sweetens the chalices of our penitence; it is the signature of Christ's blood which gives value to what would be worthless paper in our soul's sorrow; it is the Heart of Christ which heals the contrite of heart.

Chapter Five

∞

Christ's pierced Heart heals your wounded heart

"Bring hither thy hand,
and put it into my side."

John 20:27

∞

One kind of a heart wound is inflicted by the loss of those we love. The separation may be brought about by estrangement or by death, and who shall say which wound is deeper or more painful? Who sorrowed more: the widow of Naim[28] or the father of the prodigal?[29] Now, Christ's Heart was wounded so that ours may be healed. He says to every heart, "Peace be to thee,"[30] and invites every sorrowing soul, as He did St. Thomas, to find its solace in His open side. "Bring hither thy hand, and put it into my side."

Death indeed has its sorrows, and sharp is the edge of its reaping hook. In many a home, the voice once heard is heard no more; its echoes have died away. The eyes that glistened there with the regret of a daily departure, the smile that flashed a daily welcome with unfailing brightness — these have disappeared in gloom, and those of the household look and listen in vain. A well-known step sounds no more on the stairway, and the chair in the family circle, vacant forever, is a sad companion in the gathering twilight. Yet, even that wound will be closed by the healing touch of time and by the

[28] Luke 7:11-15.
[29] Luke 15:11-32.
[30] John 20:19.

blessed forgetfulness that comes with new duties and new affections.

The tomb is final, and, bad as it is, we know the worst. But the wound of separation stays open longer. Estrangement is a daily death and is ever presenting to the mind new fears, more dreaded prospects. The heart made vacant by a death may be filled again with new growth, but the desert sands of living separation put forth no blooms to refresh the aching gaze. The widow's son is at rest in the graveyard, where she may go and pray, but the prodigal's father is ever on the torturing rack with rumors of riotous living and famine and disgrace and filth and starvation, and is oppressed by the darkening despair that the prodigal, as often happens, will never come home.

It may be hard, or even impossible, to determine which of these two wounds of loss — death or estrangement — is more painful, but there can be no doubt that another kind of heart wound, the wound of pride, gives the keenest of all tortures. The heart wounded by pride often develops a festering sore. It does not — and will tell you that it *cannot* — forget, as those bereaved by death can do. Pride is, in reality, the cause of the worst anguish in estrangement, because what chafes in such separations is the thought that other persons have been preferred to us.

The wounds of pride fester because a poison has tainted the weapon that made them. If a humble heart is wounded, it is not surprised. It does not identify itself with the universe, does not consider itself the crowned king of creation. But for the proud heart, every affront or quarrel or humiliation is an offense against kingly majesty. The wound may be concealed; it refuses to be cured. To be cured, pride must go out of itself, and it would not be pride if it did that. Humility feels the hurt, but it does not feel hurt. Pride transfers the wound to personality; it recognizes a defeat; it smarts from another's superiority. In a football game, the ball is only a distraction, while twenty-two souls and bodies grapple for mastery; the real issue of endurance and tactics could be determined just as well with a pincushion or a rope's end. In like manner, in a heart wounded by pride, the real issue is not the word said or the deed done, but the fact that one king is rolling in the dust and feels the heel of another upon his neck. That feeling is the poison which festers; that is the heart wound which does not heal.

∞

"Bring hither thy hand, and put it into my side." So says the Heart of Christ risen from the dead. Christ went about consoling His stricken ones during the days that followed His Resurrection.

Mark His wonderful condescension, King Pride, you who are enthroned in the wounded heart; mark how He submits to the conditions imposed by Thomas, how He humbly bows to His follower's haughty, "I will not!"

It is the evidence and practice of God to draw good from evil. Never was there a more striking instance than here. Would we ever have known that the way into Christ's Heart was open except for Thomas's lack of faith? Perhaps not. At all events, there is no doubt about it now, that, when Christ glorified His body, He did not remove His wounds, but kept them to console us.

The first stage in the consoling of wounded hearts by the Heart of Christ is the restoring of faith. "Bring hither thy hand, and put it into my side; and be not faithless but believing." A wound is not a reason for loss of faith in man and God. The wound of Christ is a proof of His divinity. Christ has not promised that our hearts will not be wounded, but He has proved that our wounds will be our glory; He has proved that if we go down into the dark hollows on the sea of sorrow, we shall mount again to the heights of joy. The trough of the wave of Calvary rose to the white crest of Easter.

The Heart of Christ is the healing of wounded hearts, because He has traveled all the ways of loss and separation. We can enter upon no path of sorrow where His Cross has not cast its shadow, where His feet have not left footprints of blood. He entered, too, into the valley of death. His body was made, it could be said, for immediate immortality, unlike ours, which must pass through dust to immortality. So, besides the deaths which, throughout His life, wounded His Heart — the death of St. Joseph and of Lazarus and of many others — His own death, the separation of His soul from His body, gave Him the sharpest of wounds, and it was especially hard for His Heart to die, because death was not its due.

There was, then, no wound of death which His Heart did not feel, and there was no wound of estrangement which He was not called upon to suffer. He felt the exile from friends in Egypt.[31] If Mary and Joseph sought Him sorrowing before they found Him in the Temple, much more did He sorrow staying away from them.[32] These were but shallow wounds if measured beside the gashes of His Passion, when His people abandoned

[31] Matt. 2:13-14.
[32] Luke 2:48.

Him and His Apostles, when, by His own wish, His mother was forced to abandon Him, and when, finally — deepest of all wounds of estrangement — the cry was wrung from His lips: "My God, my God, why hast Thou forsaken me?"[33]

"So, you also who have a heart wounded by a humiliation, bring it here, and put it into my side," Christ says to us all. "I, who am true King and God of all, have been humbled to the dust. The hand behind the spearpoint was one to which I was reaching out my hand, that I might grasp it in love and lift a soul to Heaven. Many would have festering heart wounds if the one to whom they gave a cup of water would cast it in derision into their face. I gave of the brimming contents of my Heart, and mocking insulters have flung my unavailing blood back upon me.

"More than that, wounded heart, the very blow which festers within you fell upon my Heart. This is no exaggeration, no figure of speech. I died for all sins and for the selfsame sin that wounded your heart, and because I know God better and understand sin more fully, and because, too, I love you better than you do yourself, the wound that was dealt you was dealt to me and gave me more intense pain than it did or could possibly give to you. Bring here, then, your heart, whether wounded by loss or humiliation, and put it into my side, and you will find there a Heart more deeply wounded."

---

[33] Matt. 27:46.

Chapter Six

Christ's Heart is the source of holiness

"From the heart come
forth evil thoughts."

Matthew 15:19

∞

Holiness is of the heart. When that truth was obscured and almost forgotten, Christ made it clear and certain. Christ our Savior is likewise the Savior of man's heart. The Pharisees had made saintliness an external thing, a matter of ceremony and routine. Christ did not condemn the externals, but He placed the saintliness within. He put a heart behind the ceremony.

On one occasion, among many, Christ asserted the dignity of man's heart in the strong language which characterized His teaching against the Pharisees. They had complained, "Why do Thy disciples transgress the traditions of the ancients? For they wash not their hands when they eat bread."[34] Christ made answer, "Not that which goeth into the mouth defileth a man, but what cometh out of the mouth, this defileth a man. . . . The things which proceed out of the mouth come forth from the heart. For from the heart come forth evil thoughts, murders, adulteries, fornications, thefts, false testimonies, blasphemies. These are the things that defile a man. But to eat with unwashed hands doth not defile a man."[35]

"Out of the heart" are the momentous words that proclaim a far-reaching principle, a revolution in morals, an emancipation

[34] Matt. 15:2.
[35] Matt. 15:11, 18-20.

from traditional slavery, a declaration of independence from mere formalities. "Out of the heart" transferred morals from manners to man, from the hand to the heart. The heart makes an act good or evil, because the heart is free, and man should be more anxious about cleansing the heart than washing the hands.

Christ's purpose must not be misunderstood. He no more condemned fasting here than He approved of gluttony. His purpose was to refer holiness to its proper source, to restore the heart to its lawful throne. Fasting may be holiness, or it may be hypocrisy, and it is the heart that makes the difference. Nor does Christ condemn the washing of hands. To wash the hands may be an aid to holiness, but it will not constitute holiness. Christ did not wish to abolish ceremonies; He wished to abolish superstition and formalism and hypocrisy. He desired to restore circulation to the heart, and then there would be adoration in spirit and truth, united with the appropriate expression of both in word, in garb, and in ritual.

The purpose, then, of Christ was to put the emphasis on the right place. There is tremendous significance in the words "out of the heart." They designate, in the case of sin, an act of man's free will, deliberately choosing evil instead of good, or making the choice out of an evil motive, or permitting the act of the will to lack its due perfection. The person who dips his hand into the mud with evil intent to cast it upon another person, has a soiled object, a soiled hand, and a soiled purpose. Out of the heart may come deeds thrice stained: stained because the heart's object may be evil; stained because the heart's action may be evil, like the soiled fingers; and stained because the heart's motive may be evil. Out of the heart may come deeds bearing but one of these stains, yet teeming with dread consequences.

It is that standard of morality set by Christ which makes all the difference in the world, or, rather, which makes an eternal difference. No detail of life that comes within the scope of man's free will escapes the influence of the heart. Every detail comes from a saintly or a sinful heart and bears with it the seeds of everlasting consequences.

Suppose a man builds a monument. How long will it perpetuate his name? For a few years only. But out of the heart come monuments untouched by the ruinous finger of time. Man can send his thoughts and his voice over the land and across the sea. What comes out of the heart reaches a wire which sends man's soul over the wide chasm of the grave into the unending depths of Heaven or Hell. Christ restored freedom to man's heart, but He did not take away the heart's responsibility.

The Heart of Christ: who shall measure the richness, the saintliness issuing from that sacred source? The Fathers of the Church tell us that the Church was born out of the Heart of Christ on the Cross,[36] as Eve was born out of the side of Adam. The water and blood were the sacraments of Baptism and Holy Eucharist — striking picture of a more striking reality!

Out of Christ's Heart came the sanctification of mankind. It is the brimming ocean of all our holiness. The grace won by His opened Heart serves to purify our hearts. Every thought,

[36] John 19:34.

word, or deed, freed from the triple stain of sinful object, sinful act, and sinful end, and bright with the corresponding triple good, lacks the evil and rejoices in the good because of Christ's opened heart. There is not the tiniest atom of holiness in the universe which does not reveal to the microscopic gaze of faith a tinge of the blood which passed through the Heart of Christ.

The Heart of Christ is holy because it is the cause of all created holiness, and, further, it is holy in itself. Christ was God and, as such, infinitely holy in many ways, and especially in the way of purest love. Sin is the embracing of evil by the heart; sinlessness is the embracing of good, and infinite sinlessness is the love of infinite good. God's holiness is infinite because His love is infinitely pure. Its object is God Himself; its motive is God; and there is no stopping short of infinite purity in the perfection of the act of love in itself. In God, love measures up to the level of His knowledge of Himself. The will which loves will love as intensely and as extensively as it knows, and, in God, the knowledge of Himself is infinite. The object, the motive, and the act may be stained in human love; in God, they are all infinitely pure, and His holiness is infinite.

Christ, as man, participated of the holiness of God. We are indeed made holy by the vesting of our souls with God's grace. That created gift of God makes us, as St. Peter says, "partakers of the divine nature."[37] What, then, must be the holiness of Christ, to whose human nature God Himself is united, not by the unstable bond of grace, but by the union, permanent and intimate, of His Second Person. And mark! Christ was not

[37] 2 Pet. 1:4.

denied the fullness of created grace. He was to be the perennial source of all created holiness, and "of His fullness we all have received."[38] The Heart of Christ is holy by union with the infinitely holy Person of God, and holy with as much grace as a created soul is capable of.

We are bewildered with the splendor of this holiness. Our eyes are fixed on the central fiery core of an unblemished sun, where the trace of an imperfection could not survive for a moment in the purging whiteness of love's purest heat. We are watching the flames that blend and rise to God from the Heart of Christ. No wonder artists have crowned that Heart with a blaze of light and pictured it as consumed in its own splendor.

The observance of law is the test of love, as it is the expression of holiness. "If you love me, keep my commandments."[39] This is Christ's own test, and fully does His Heart measure up to it. The law is the manifestation of the will of the lawgiver, and holiness is found in abiding by that will. The ineffably pure affection of Christ's Heart loves God for the sake of God alone, and loves Him perfectly. God's commandments become the commandments of Christ's Heart, for love makes the will of the lawgiver the will of the lover. And so law is transformed and passes into its perfect state in that fervent fusion of love's making; law becomes love, and love becomes law. So it is in the saintly Heart of Christ, and so it is in every saintly heart that is modeled after His.

---

[38] John 1:16.
[39] John 14:15.

Chapter Seven

∞

Christ's Heart speaks
words of power

"Out of the abundance
of the heart . . ."

Matthew 12:34

Artists and people of artistic tastes may pay close attention to the wreaths and eagles and heads stamped on our coins, but the practical businessman looks to the coin's metal and purchasing power. We are all minting daily a multitude of coins, and the angel treasurers of the vaults of Heaven do not spend as much time looking for our profiles and the dates on these coins as they do in sounding the metal to test if it rings true and will pass as currency in the kingdom of Heaven.

Christ was a keen merchant in the business of the soul. Witness His parables, and see that buying and selling had no mysteries for Him. So, when the Pharisees would pass off their worthless money upon Him, He knew the counterfeit at once and cried, "O generation of vipers, how can you speak good things whereas you are evil? For out of the abundance of the heart, the mouth speaketh."[40]

"There will not be gold on the lips if there is not gold in the heart" is Christ's teaching. The rich heart makes the rich word. "Out of the abundance of the heart" means "out of the riches of the heart," and this is clear from the signification of the word in the original text and from the words that follow: "A good man, out of a good treasure, bringeth forth good things;

---

[40] Matt. 12:34.

an evil man, out of an evil treasure, bringeth forth evil things."[41]
The words may be artistic; they may be colored with poetry,
warmed with eloquence, or freighted with the rarest knowledge. All that is mere mintage and tinsel, not itself precious
metal in the sight of God. It need not necessarily be base metal
either, but its purchasing value in the mart of Heaven will not
be greater than would a double eagle made of golden butter,
unless the treasure of the heart goes with the treasures of art.

Before men, we may all pass for the character in the fairy
tale, dropping pearls and diamonds and silver and gold every
time our lips part, but what of the output of the heart before
the eyes of God? May not the words be paste and pewter and
brass, or, at the best, lightly plated ware?

The question is a serious one. One day, a collection shall
be made of all our treasures and their values estimated. "But I
say unto you," continues the Lord, "that every idle word that
men shall speak they shall render an account of."[42] There is a
very dismal prospect indeed! To think that all our idle words,
the fleeting sounds into which we have put vain, fleeting
thoughts, all that foam and froth of the stream of speech, is entered against us. Alas, poor lips that babble on heedlessly, of
you we may say in the words of the Lord, slightly changed,
"Out of the abundance of the mouth, the heart is silent." Idle
words are the product of silent hearts.

No man can say with the sinners in the psalm, "Our lips are
our own. Who is lord over us?"[43] Unhappily, our lips are not

[41] Matt. 12:35.
[42] Matt. 12:36.
[43] Ps. 11:5 (RSV = Ps. 12:4).

our own. God made them, and they are His and must work for Him. An idle word is one that refuses to recognize God's ownership. Let the heart admit God's mastery; let the intention of doing all for God's services be renewed occasionally, and words will cease to be idle.

There is, then, no need here of disturbing worry. The good Christian, trying to lead a good life, is by that very fact banishing idle words. Morning and evening prayers, offering the day to God, Mass, acts of piety and charity: all these are evidences of a rich heart, out of which come few or no idle words. The mother who loves her child never utters an idle word in his regard, because in every word is the refined gold of love. Every Christian who loves God has a heart rich in love and is rarely idle in words.

Who can estimate the richness of the Heart of Christ? It is the incarnation of the love of God. "The love of God was made Heart, and throbbed among us," we may say, following the words and spirit of St. John.[44] The Heart of Christ is the symbol, the representation, of the love of Christ, and so of the love of God. "God so loved the world as to give His only-begotten Son."[45] The ripest fruit of divine love, we may say, interpreting these words, was the Incarnation. The Heart of Christ was created to put before us the love of God in a language we could understand. God so loved that He gave. What, then, are the treasures of Christ's Heart? They are the richness

[44] Cf. John 1:14.
[45] John 3:16.

of Christ's love as God and the richness of Christ's love as man. The beating of His Heart voiced both loves.

Consider, then, what was the precious coinage of Christ's lips. We may judge from their power. His words were omnipotent. They spoke to blind eyes, and they saw; to deaf ears, and they heard; to dumb tongues, and they spoke. "Peace, be still,"[46] He said to the waves, and they fell to sleep. "Be thou clean,"[47] He said to the leper, and his flesh at once grew wholesome, and firm, and ruddy with the glow of health. His words were stronger still, "more piercing than any two-edged sword; and reaching into the divisions of the soul and spirit; and discerners of the thoughts and intents of the heart."[48] The sinful and sorrowful heard His words, and sin and sadness were sloughed off the soul like the scales of leprosy from the body.

Truly, Christ's words were like a two-edged sword, edged with divine and human love! Every action of Christ was one because it was the action of one person, but it was twofold in being accompanied by the action of His human and divine nature. The white-hot sword, so the old theologians put it, will cut and will burn, but who will separate the section of the metal which cuts from the section which burns? Every part burns; every part cuts. So in the fire of Christ's word are blended the flames of two loves. In the beating of His heart, the ear can detect the harmony of two sounds: the melody of the greatest love that ever throbbed in man, and its harmonic melody of infinitely higher octaves, the love of God. Every

[46] Mark 4:39.
[47] Matt. 8:3.
[48] Heb. 4:12.

word, then, of Christ was far from idleness. It was possessed of a divine and infinite energy. It was the coinage of the gold of Christ's Heart.

Today we hear the same words; we witness and experience their might. The words of Christ are now on the lips of Christ's priests. "I absolve you," says the priest, imparting by those words of Christ the precious treasure of grace to the souls of men. "This is my Body," says the priest, speaking in the person of Christ. Immediately, by the transmuting power of the words of Christ, the crushed and baked wheat, poor, cheap substance that it is, is transformed into substance infinitely surpassing earth's rarest ores. Thus do all the sacraments, every moment of every day, reveal everywhere to mankind the supreme richness of the Heart of Christ by the enriching words of Christ.

Chapter Eight

∞

Christ's Heart
calms your fears

"O foolish and slow of heart
to believe . . ."

Luke 24:24

Dark corners give pause to the steps of a child. What monster may be hidden in the shadows there he does not know, but the monster loses none of its terror for being imaginary and not real. The childish fancy huddles in the black gloom, having before it all the fearful things its brief experience has known, and adds to them new horrors, more towering heads, more fiery eyes and wilder looks, and rougher hands with more mysterious weapons of frightful torture. No wonder the child is slow of step when a dark corner looms up before him!

Was it not some such turn in the way of the soul, some dismal prospect peopled with apprehension, that made the two disciples turn from Jerusalem the morning of the Resurrection to their home at Emmaus and brought down upon them the rebuke, "O foolish and slow of heart to believe in all things which the prophets have spoken"?[49]

The heart of man is not far from his imagination. It will rush exultantly after fancied joys or lag reluctantly with leaden pace where the imagination has nothing but sadness and pain in view. Had this pair of saddened hearts who journeyed to Emmaus relied on faith rather than imagination, they would not have shrunk from the disgrace of Calvary or the fear of the

[49] Luke 24:25.

Jews who opposed Jesus. Faith could have told them that if there had been no Calvary, Christ could not have been the Messiah; that their disappointed hopes rested on a belief in some but not all of the things which the prophets had spoken; that the risen Savior was on the way to the supper room where the Apostles and disciples were gathered, just at the very time they themselves were leaving it.

In every heart, there is a struggle between the swiftness of faith and the slowness of nature. Every act of the soul that merits the vision of God springs into being at the voice of faith. If I practice temperance in drinking for no other motive than to avoid ruining my apparel by falling into the gutter, my virtue is natural and has its natural reward: I save my hat. But if I wish to have the reward of God, I must be temperate because He told me that "drunkards shall not possess the kingdom of God."[50] If I obey nature, I receive my pay from nature; if I hearken to the voice of God, I shall merit a recompense from Him exceedingly great. So every thought or word or act that is to end in Heaven and in God begins in faith.

Ah, but nature is near to the soul and is always advertising its rewards. The imagination is its advertising agency, and never were wares more temptingly described than by that agency — never more striking type for display, never more catchy engravings, never such flattering assurances of the best results. What will faith do to offset the nearness of nature and its alluring advertisements? How shall a man "stagger not in his heart but believe,"[51] when virtue seems gloomy, when the

---

[50] Cf. 1 Cor. 6:10.
[51] Mark 11:23.

shades of the open confessional appear to be filled with horrible monsters, or when the voice of vocation calls the soul along the way of poverty, chastity, and obedience at the very time when, with a more clamorous insistence, the advantages of riches, indulgence, and license call to him? The promptness of love must spur the hearts that are slow to believe all.

∞

"Behold, I come"[52] was the swift reply of God the Son to the call of His Father. "Sacrifices and oblations and holocausts for sin Thou wouldst not," wrote the psalmist and St. Paul of our Lord. "Then said I, 'Behold, I come, to do Thy will, O God.' "[53] That cry of promptness created the Heart of Christ. Its first beat was an echo of that generous offering. The Heart of Christ, then, will lend wings to the slow of heart.

Yet, it may be urged that the Heart of Christ had the vision of the Father, and so had the inexhaustible wealth of charity, but had not the virtue of faith. Very true it is "that we see now through a glass in a dark manner," but Christ saw "face-to-face."[54] He had not the difficulty of obscurity that vexes our hearts in faith, but He had such a consuming fire of love and obedience as would have swept off in its rapidity a thousand greater difficulties, had they come into His way. It is no reproach to the sun that its splendor is not dimmed by the smoke from a wick, which is enough to obscure the flame of the candle. Christ had all the excellence of faith in the perfection, the

---

[52] Heb. 10:7.
[53] Ps. 39:7-9 (RSV = Ps. 40:6-8); Heb. 10:5-7.
[54] 1 Cor. 13:12.

promptness, and the generous completeness of His surrender to the will of the Father: "Behold, I come."

Witness how all through life, Christ was prompt in the face of obstacles which usually make us slow of heart to believe. Faith calls upon us to make what might be termed a plunge into the dark, although faith is rather a lifting on high in a flawless, unfailing, and unfalling vessel of Heaven. But if faith is fancied to be a plunge, then the Heart of Christ plunged from above down to the nothingness of man.

When the lights and music were attractive at Bethlehem, His Heart passed rather into the darkness of the cave and the lowliness of the manger. No unholy love could taint His Heart or make it slow to respond when God's voice spoke, but the perfect tenderness of His pure love for His mother made the promptness of His sacrifice more keenly felt when He left her to be about the business of His Father in the Temple of Jerusalem or throughout the lands of Judea and Galilee. No sinful imagination could soil Him with seductive prospects, but His Heart was not slow when, in His agony in Gethsemane, the more piercing vision of His mind brought before Him and upon Him the weight of all mankind's iniquity.

Christ's agony was truly a struggle, a resistance unto blood, to comfort us when the night of passion oppresses our weakness. It was a struggle that printed itself in blood-red letters for our reading. Yet the heart was true, was prompt when the test finally came: "Behold, I come to do Thy will, O God"; "not my will, but Thine be done." So, finally, in the last dark moments of Christ's life, when a heavier weight than sin fell upon His Heart, there was the same promptness, and the Heart which cried out as though God had forsaken it shook off, if we may so speak, the slowness that dark desolation would have put upon it, and confidently and peacefully commended itself into the Father's hands, a short while before the hands of men laid open with a spear that treasure-house of quick, generous love.

The heart of man may be compared to a wave of the sea. What a restless creature is a wave! Who can balance one drop of water upon another? Who, then, can keep a million jostling, smooth, slipping, tiny crystal spheres quiet for the briefest fraction of a moment? And then the air, with its multitude of shifting particles ever in ceaseless agitation — who can keep all that in rest when the lifting of an eyelash will disturb it? Now, bring the fickle air out over the waters, and let it play upon that liquid restlessness, and you have a wave of the sea.

St. James took that wave as an image of a heart without faith. "Let them ask in faith, nothing wavering. For he that wavereth is like a wave of the sea, which is moved and carried about by the winds."[55] The heart of man is no calmer than the surface of the sea. Over it sweeps a host of feelings which keep it ever surging here and there and forever pausing upon the verge of some new direction. Sorrows and delights, fears and encouragements, hates, resentments and angers, attractions, infatuations and passions, whirl like shifting winds over the heart.

However, what tames the unstable wave and makes it sway in one direction will also give steadiness to the heart — a principle from on high. Far off in the sky, the moon swings around in a circle and the great ocean moves in obedience to its mighty power.

---

[55] James 1:6.

How to Love as Jesus Loves

The promptness of faith or love will make the unquiet currents of the heart docile and steady and quickly responsive. Loving obedience to the will of the Father made the Heart of Christ swift to hearken and act, and trusting obedience to the voice of God will prevent our infinitely weaker hearts from being slow to believe and act when a thousand agitations would swerve us from the right. The heart of Christ is a spur to the slow of heart.

Chapter Nine

∞

You are the treasure of Christ's Heart

"Where thy treasure is,
there is thy heart also."

Matthew 6:21

∞

Love was and is the first and greatest monopolist. The heart and the heart's object tend to union; they are jealous of any intrusion that would interfere with that intimate union; they form a closed circle and a closed circuit, through which the current of affection passes from loving to loved.

The monopoly is not formed and completed at once. According to the teaching of our Lord, there are three main stages in the process: the transfer of the heart, the transfer of the mind, and the transfer of all the rest. When Christ issued His warning against avarice and against making riches the object of love, He said that where the treasure is, there also shall be the heart, that the light within a person becomes darkness, and that the lover of wealth becomes the slave of mammon. Heart, mind, and all are consigned to the treasure, and the monopoly is formed. The soul is enticed, entranced, and enslaved.

For each stage, Christ uttered a warning. Before you are enticed, before you lose your heart, consider the contrast between the treasures of earth and Heaven. Moths, rust, and thieves destroy the treasures of earth.[56] Beauty has its enemies as well as wealth. Disease is the moth that preys upon the fair

---

[56] Cf. Matt. 6:19.

face, age will rust the charms of youth, and death is the thief that is no respecter of the handsome form. Moths will attack the king's robes, and rust will eat up the king's crown, and usurpers and successors will steal away his throne.

Wealth, beauty, and power are not safety-deposits for human hearts. There is only one place in the universe where mothballs, rust removers, and burglar alarms are not needed. If you are to be enticed into parting with your heart, our Lord warns you to put it where it will not be moth-eaten or devoured by rust or carried away by thieves. Since the heart will follow the treasures, it will suffer their fate. "Lay up for ourselves treasures in Heaven."[57]

The wish is father to the thought and has, it might be added, a very large family. Can the pale clerk cooped up in the city remain long at the seaside without being tanned? Can the Eskimo take off his furs without feeling cold? The questions would be easy in the kindergarten, and in the class of physics, the scholars would say that heat radiates constantly until all the environment becomes of the same temperature. What, then, will become of a pale, anemic mind when subjected to a blazing heart, or a thinly clothed mind when exposed to an arctic heart? The mind assumes the temperature of the heart. To say that the mind is a thermometer to the heart is only another way of saying that the wish is father to the thought.

If the heart loves the cashbox, the mind will not love the poor box. The heart, by which I mean the will with its desires, will bring the thoughts its way. Entrancement will follow enticement, or, as our Lord puts it, entering His warning against

[57] Matt. 6:20.

this second stage of an illegal monopoly: "If the light that is within thee is darkness, the darkness itself — how great shall it be!"[58] His meaning is that the mind is the eye of the soul, and whatever blinds it, blinds the soul. Passion and entice-ment — in a word, the heart buried in treasures — eclipse the sight of the mind. "There are no ugly loves," someone has said. The loving heart keeps the rarest cosmetics for the object of its love. The mind, therefore, is bewitched, infatuated, and en-tranced. The doom pronounced by Christ against this second advance in the process of evil love is darkness, and he hesi-tates to specify its intense blackness. "The darkness — how great shall it be!"

The last stage of love's degradation is enslavement. "No man can serve two masters."[59] This is the solemn warning of Christ. Where a man's heart and mind are, there also shall be the rest of him. There does not seem to be any place for bimetalism in the human heart. The single standard rules there: the gold of God or the gold of earth. A river cannot flow north and south at the same time. When the heart's currents wear out a channel for themselves and develop an impetus, who will turn back the strong floods? Some saints have been known to have bilocated, or been in two places at once. The heart cannot bilocate. If it is heaped over with gold and swathed in greenbacks, it is not kneeling in sackcloth and ashes before God. A man may have both riches and God, but he cannot serve both. He cannot belong to two nationalities or to two opposite political parties. If he is of the race of God

[58] Matt. 6:23.
[59] Matt. 6:24.

and an upholder of the views of God, he is not of the race of mammon and his adherent. Therefore, Christ's solemn warning to the enticed and infatuated heart is exhorting it to avoid enslavement: "You cannot serve both God and mammon."[60]

∞

We have gone down to the depths of love, or, to use a more proper term, to the depths of passion. It is passion, more than love, which should be called the monopolist. Love deserves a term of more noble memories and associations. Love is a conqueror and a king.

Having, then, studied the degradation of passion, we now ascend to the lofty, glorious heights of love. It was in eternity and in God that love was born. There it had infinite good and infinite beauty to contemplate and cling to, but even that seemed hardly enough for King Love, the conqueror. It longed for other kingdoms. It would have another treasure also and a heart to put with it, and love created both. The heart was the Heart of Christ, the creation of divine love, and we were the treasures. The souls of men, which have their moths and rust and thieves — the souls of men, with coldness, neglect, and sin — were the treasures of the Second Person of the Blessed Trinity.

When Christ spoke of the passion of man, of man's having his heart in his treasures, He spoke in a figurative way. It was a striking phrase which told that man always longs for his treasures. But the Incarnation, when God created the Heart of Christ, was the realization of the first stage of advancing love.

[60] Matt. 6:24.

Where Christ's soul treasures were, there also His Heart really came to be. "My delight is to be with the sons of men."[61]

In the Incarnation was the first victory of love; in the Passion was the second. If human passion has its infatuation, so, too, has true love. The way the blood of Christ's Heart throbbed to burst forth and be shed for us, His statement that He had a baptism of blood to be baptized with and was straitened until it should be accomplished,[62] His eagerness, which outstripped the Apostles on the way to Jerusalem, the lavishness with which He poured out blood where one drop would do and with which He permitted a host of varied torments when one pang of one pain would have been enough for our salvation: these are all overwhelming proofs that His love had reached the heights of divine infatuation and merited to be termed the "folly of the Cross."[63] The light of His heart was not darkened, as the light of earthly passion grows dark in its second stage. His light was resplendent, and, adapting His words, we may say, "If the light that is in thee be splendor, the splendor itself — how great shall it be!"

One would imagine that with the two conquests of the Incarnation and the Passion, love had extended its kingdom far enough. But no! Holy love has its slavery too, if we may call it that, although it would be truer to call it consecration. Love has always been a uniter, but the Heart of Christ has revealed to us unheard-of powers under this aspect. His Heart leaped the chasm that yawned between divinity and humanity, and

---

[61] Prov. 8:31.
[62] Luke 12:50.
[63] 1 Cor. 1:18.

united them. The Incarnation was the first wonderful union of love.

Christ's Heart devised yet another union with His treasures, the hearts of men, which staggers the belief and demands the testimony of God to establish its truth. What union is that? It is the union that He effects by His abiding presence in the Holy Eucharist and His intimate presence within us in Communion. No slave ever put himself so completely at the will of His master as Christ does for us. No love for men or for money brings about an actual physical incorporation between the heart and its object.

The Heart of Christ, then, has attained to the highest heights of love. It enslaves itself in the bonds of wine and wheat; it becomes our food and drink. It serves both God and men. Can love do more? The "folly" of Good Friday and the daily consecration upon the altar are the triumphs and the climax of love's conquest in the Heart of Christ!

Chapter Ten

∞

*Christ enkindles
in your heart
the flame of love*

"Was not our heart
burning within us?"

Luke 24:31

Many find it hard to get over disappointment. If others disappoint them, they note the fact down, say it over to themselves often during the day, stay awake thinking over it at night, and make themselves generally miserable for a long time. If they are disappointed in themselves, the disease is worse, and it sometimes reaches a crisis in suicide.

Self-disappointment is a subtle form of pride. In the innermost recesses of consciousness is a little shrine, fragrant with the incense of self-gratification, illuminated with the lights of achievements that are great in the person's view and brilliant with the gathered bouquets of hoarded compliments. These are the furnishings of the shrine, and they are grouped reverentially about the golden statue of self. The shrine has one persistent worshiper, whose knees never weary.

But one fine day, as the sole worshiper turns at early dawn to his adoration, the thought of a failure occurs — a clear, undeniable failure. Will not a thicker cloud of incense hide it from view? Alas, it would, except for one thing: others know of the failure. Self has not come up to its own expectations, and the world knows it.

Look at the shrine! The incense is merely burning rubber; the candles are smoking wicks. Take the flowers away; the golden statue is that of a calf, like the one worshiped by the

Israelites in the desert.[64] Thus this religion of self-worship, with its high priest, temple, and ritual, passes into dust forever. If there is humility near, a better, truer religion will be built upon the ruins; if pride rules, there is lamentation and the loss of all religion.

There is a notable instance of self-disappointment in the Gospels that had a more fortunate ending than is usual in cases of the kind. It surely was a sorrowful and gloomy group of Apostles and disciples which gathered together in shivering silence in Jerusalem after Christ, their leader, had been condemned as a traitor and a malefactor and killed. They were the coldhearted remnants of a lost cause. "We hoped" was their cry. The gorgeous sunset in which they had basked had suddenly become a very thick, very disagreeable, and very chilling fog when the Sun of Justice had set behind the hills. "We hoped" is the cry of self-disappointment, the lament of a cold, dark heart.

Among that crowd were two whose hearts had become lumps of ice. "Away from Jerusalem," said their cold hearts, "and back to Emmaus!" They had heard whispers around them of the body of their Master not being found, but their cold hearts urged that these were tales of women, frightened and trying to frighten them, that it was before the light and that those early risers had seen a vision.[65] "We hoped" quenched all their faith, all their humility. They had constructed a brilliant plan upon which the universe was to be managed hereafter. Divine Providence had not seen fit to conform to their view,

[64] Cf. Exod. 32:4.
[65] Luke 24:22-23.

and their hearts were disappointed and cold, without faith, without humility, without hope.

∞

Our Lord had come to send fire upon earth.[66] He surely needed a good fire as He drew near the cold hearts of the travelers to Emmaus. But the ice was turned into a flame after being brought into contact with the divine Heart of Christ. When "their eyes were held"[67] and they failed to recognize our Lord, their hearts were cold; but when "their eyes were opened"[68] and they recognized Him, they confessed that their hearts were burning: "Was not our heart burning within us, whilst He spoke upon the way?"[69] His Heart was the furnace in which their icy hearts had been placed and had been melted and inflamed once more to faith, hope, and humility.

But this was not done all at once. A sudden transportation from the arctic to the torrid zone would be violent. That was not how the Heart of Jesus worked. He came upon the hearts of these travelers to Emmaus with the steady, melting, almost imperceptible force of the spring. They had humility enough to let Jesus draw near and so merited the greater humility of confessing their condition. They listened humbly. He brought them to see that their hopes were childish, that the Messiah was too large for Palestine, too great for a kingdom of earth, and that the death which had chilled their hearts was the very

[66] Cf. Luke 12:49.
[67] Luke 24:16.
[68] Luke 24:31.
[69] Luke 24:32.

proof that He was the Messiah, the very battle which won Him His true kingdom. "Ought not Christ to have suffered these things and so have entered into His glory?"[70]

They went out from the dictation of self and let themselves be taught. And their humility went further: they were willing to depend upon another. Here before them was a religious teacher who was building for them a better shrine of enduring hopes, and they humbled themselves to prayer.

"Stay with us, because it is toward evening and the day is far spent."[71] There was to be one more step in their progress. Jesus drew near them. They welcomed Him and kept Him near. To bring the full force of His Heart upon theirs, He should come still nearer: "He took bread, and blessed and broke and gave it to them."[72] With their hearts beside His Heart, they needed no longer His presence before their eyes. "Away from Emmaus," was their cry, prompt and resolute, "and back to Jerusalem."

It was our Lord's will to ransom us in the way of justice, to pay the price for us. His Heart consoles us in disappointment, because He experienced the keenest pangs of disappointment. We shall have no path of sorrow on which to tread in life where we cannot see the red footprints of the Savior.

Naturally, Christ felt the exultation of success. His Heart exulted in joy, but it was at times depressed in sadness. His triumphal entry into Jerusalem marked the highest point of His exultation. The very stones, He said, would take voices and

[70] Luke 24:25.
[71] Luke 24:29.
[72] Luke 24:30.

acclaim Him.[73] The world is wreathed in smiles for the exultant heart and dances with its dancing. That sunshine of Christ's glory is noonday whiteness when set in contrast with the midnight blackness of His disappointment. His Heart, when it sent forth that agonizing cry, "My God, my God, why hast Thou forsaken me?"[74] was not in despair, yet it was deeper down in blacker disappointment than that which has sent many a weaker heart to suicide.

In that hour, Christ's Heart paid the price of our consolation. It traversed the bleak and barren fields of arctic cold, and as its weakness became our strength, so its coldness became our warmth. There was kindled the fire He came to cast upon earth, fire to melt away the ice of pride from disappointed hearts and to fill them with flames of faith and humility, surging through the burning hearts that touch the burning Heart of Christ.

[73] Luke 19:40.
[74] Matt. 27:46.

Chapter Eleven

∞

Christ gives you His complete love and attention

"Let not your heart
be troubled."

John 14:1

An eclipse of the sun is full of terrors for those who do not know its nature. The high position, the lordly movement, the warmth, the splendor, and the magnificence of the sun have made it a god for some minds. To see, then, that resplendent orb and its universal flood of daylight blotted out of the sky by a mysterious shadow could not fail to disturb and terrify its worshipers.

Our Lord is the Sun of Justice, the Light of the World, and the true God. For three years, He had filled the lives of His followers, so on the night before His Crucifixion, as they saw and felt the shadows of death upon Him, no wonder their hearts were troubled. The mysterious solemnity of the Last Supper weighed them down; the betrayal of Judas had been revealed, the denial of Peter predicted, and the departure of Jesus proclaimed;[75] and their hearts shuddered as the light seemed to be shorn from Jesus as He entered the eclipse of the tomb.

Christ knew the trouble of the Apostles, and He offered them the remedy for it. O troubled hearts of the world, hearken to the peaceful words of Christ!

St. John has kept for us the whole treatise on troubled hearts. "Let not your heart be troubled," Christ says at the

---

[75] Cf. John 13:21-26, 33, 37-38.

beginning of the fourteenth chapter of St. John's Gospel, and later He says again, "Let not your heart be troubled, nor let it be afraid."[76] Jesus furnishes His followers, one after another, with motives of consolation. The Father's mansions prepared for them, Christ's second coming, their following after Him, the gift of miracles left to them, the promise of the Paraclete, the indwelling of the Father, the peace of Christ which the world cannot give[77] — these are a few of the sources of consolation Jesus points out to the troubled hearts before Him.

But why enumerate and count the reasons for consolation? They are all combined in one sufficient and satisfying reason: the person of Christ. He is the calm of every trouble; He is the answer to every difficulty.

Christ began His farewell discourse to His Apostles with love: "Love one another as I have loved you."[78] Peter was the first, as we might have imagined, whose troubled heart voiced its difficulties. Christ replied that Peter would follow Him thereafter.[79] Thomas, as blunt if not as impulsive as Peter, was the next to cry out in trouble: "How can we know the way?" "I am the way,"[80] came the answer. Then Philip, who, on a former occasion, thought that having only a few loaves and fishes was an insuperable obstacle to feeding a multitude, once more spoke with some impatience from a too matter-of-fact mind: "Show us the Father." Christ reproachfully complains of

---

[76] John 14:27.
[77] John 14:2-3, 12, 16, 23, 27.
[78] John 13:34.
[79] John 13:36.
[80] John 14:5, 6.

Philip's lack of knowledge, but the answer is the same: "He that seeth me, seeth the Father also."[81] Judas (not Judas Iscariot) is the last to let his troubled heart find expression: "Lord, how is it that Thou will manifest Thyself to us and not to the world?" Christ had meant a spiritual manifestation, and His answer is this: since, as God, He was one with the Father, He will come to those who love Him and keep His word, and He will love them and will abide with them.[82]

One after another, the troubled hearts cry out, and in their sad cries, our own troubles find an echo. They were our spokesmen, and, in His replies through them, Christ offers Himself as the solution to every difficulty. For our distrust, He is the hope; for our wandering, He is the way; for our ignorance, the truth; for our unbelief, the fullness of belief; for our coldness, divine love; for our troubled hearts, the peace which the world cannot give. The person of Christ is the pillar of cloud by day and the pillar of fire by night when our hearts are in the desert.[83]

But why should the person of Christ be so completely the end of every way the sad heart must travel? The reasons are many. Let us dwell upon one which will show how the Heart of Christ bears with it the gift of peace. That reason is the personality of Christ's love, that is, His love for you personally. A person singles us out of many and prefers us and makes us the center upon which his heart's inclinations are focused. We are tortured by jealousy when we realize that our preference is

---

[81] John 14:8, 9.
[82] John 14:22, 23.
[83] Cf. Exod.13:21.

imperiled. But is not the recognition of that preference pride? Not where there is true love. In true love, there is a humble wonder that we should have another's affection; there is a sense and feeling of complete unworthiness that another should give place in his thoughts to us and turn his heart to us.

In the same truth is the dignity of love, as well as its preciousness. To drop personality out of view is to degrade love and doom it to a speedy destruction. Passion, selfish advantages, and mere pleasure are all signs of a mortal, passing affection.

Passion is proud; it makes itself the center and end of all. Passion is selfish; it exists only for its own gratification. One may well eat his dinner to appease someone else's appetite as make passion unselfish. But love is humble and unselfish. It goes out to another and centers upon another, not knowing, not caring, whether it will come back to self again.

In applying this teaching to the Heart of Christ, we are met with a difficulty. It is true that St. Paul, speaking of the love of Christ, declares, "He loved me and delivered Himself up for me."[84] But is that not unjustifiable egotism for St. Paul to think that Christ singled him out as an individual for His love and for the supreme test of His love? We shall see that St. Paul was not egotistical.

We must not measure the love of Christ by our imperfect standards. Christ comes to each and every one whole and entire in Communion, and the whole wealth and preference of His personality comes with Him. His Heart throbbed and shed its contents for every man, woman, and child from the first to the last, but had I been the only one in existence, there would

[84] Gal 2:20.

not have been one beat less nor one drop of blood less in the exhibition of the love of Christ's Heart.

God is a person and has personal love for us all. His love is showered from Heaven upon us individually, as if each were all. The sun would be just as bright, just as warm, if it shone on one alone, and now we all share it. Scientists tell us that, in one sense, each one sees a different sun, because the rays that lead the vision back are not the same in any two cases. Yet each and every one sees the whole sun. God's love, too, comes to each, and each can and must feel that God loves him with a personal, individual love. St. Paul was right: God loves me.

It was, however, when Christ took a heart that He made the personality of divine love tangible to us. To talk of the love of an infinite God is to talk in a somewhat unknown language. Our bodily nature is slow to understand what is spiritual and infinite. But tell us that a human heart is interested in us, and we who have had friends and a father and a mother will know at once what the personality of love means.

It is, then, in the Heart of Christ that the troubled heart will find its surest consolation, when it realizes that all of His love is centered upon it. The mother bends her head and turns her ear and listens to her child and, in that action, reveals her love. She soothes her child in sickness, and her love thrills through her touch. She looks upon her child, and the depth, intensity, and light of her eyes speak more eloquently of the ardor of her love than ear or hand, or even voice. What would men write, what convincing proof of the personality of her love would her children have if they could see her heart, which struggles for expression by means of the weak instruments of the senses?

Now, in devotion to the Heart of Christ, we are ever at the fountainhead of His love. Christ's life has become love.

Troubled heart, Christ's whole life and activity is centered upon you: He thinks of you, He listens to you, He touches you, He looks upon you, and you can know His love. His life and sufferings are before you and speak to you by His Heart, and your own heart can be filled with the joy of that preference for you. "He loves me," is the refrain that should echo above all the din of trouble.

Chapter Twelve

Christ calls you to sincerity of heart

"Their heart is far from me."

Matthew 15:8

∞

Untruth is the lack of agreement between the heart and the lips. When we say what we do not mean, we are untruthful; when we say what we do not will, we are insincere. Insincerity is vocal hypocrisy, just as hypocrisy is insincerity in action. Years ago, therefore, when Christ wished to describe the Pharisees in fit terms, He quoted Isaiah: "Well did Isaiah prophesy of you hypocrites, as it is written: This people honoreth me with their lips, but their heart is far from me."[85]

It is good to note that it is not the absence of attention, but rather the absence of *intention* that makes insincerity. Christ has not complained about the lips being far from Him, but of the heart being far from Him. If prayer or Mass or any other religious exercise is begun with the earnest desire to please God, the mere wandering of the thought from the words or acts will not make them insincere. To have insincerity, the wish itself must wander; the desire of pleasing God must be given up. If the thought flies off in any direction, the words will still ring true; the acts will not be mere acting as long as the heart turns to God. A child may play with a ball attached to a wooden paddle by a piece of elastic string. As he hits the ball with the paddle, he knows that the ball may fly off in any direction, but

[85] Cf. Matt. 15:7-8.

that it will come back and will not be lost as long as the string remains unbroken. Likewise, no matter in what direction our fickle thoughts may fly, our heart must break with God before distracted thoughts can make us insincere. The thing that should worry people in this matter is not whether the mind is distracted, but whether the heart is distracted. It is best to have both attention and intention, but it is not insincerity to have the latter without the former.

The fault of the Pharisees was that they laid all stress upon the exterior action and neglected or made little of the sincere heart. They hardly noted, or cared to note, whether it was love of God that inspired their exterior acts. The Pharisees would reduce piety to machinery. Religion would be turned into a collection of tape recordings. Some of the ancients had certain religious formulas in word or act stereotyped, and all that posterity would have to do would be to reproduce those formulas. Christ objected to reducing the service of God to the heartlessness of a tape recorder. The heart is far away from a recorded voice; Christ wanted lips and heart to be near, and the most successful automaton is no substitute in religion for the sincere heart.

∞

Christ had the sincerest of all hearts. His words rang true; they were the echo of a true heart. His Heart had in its spiritual sense, from the moment it began to beat, one and the same pulse with His Father's will, as it had in its material sense the same blood and beat with the heart of His mother. The intention of Christ never deviated from the will of His Father. "In the head of the book it was written of me: I come to do Thy will, O God,"[86] were the words on Christ's lips when His Heart began to throb. "Thy will be done"[87] were the words on Christ's lips when, obedient unto death to His Father's wishes, His Heart ceased to throb upon the Cross.

All His life, the sincerity of Christ in word and deed impressed everyone. It was, no doubt, the note of sincerity as well as the wonder of His teaching that made His hearers say that no one spoke as He did.[88] His slightest acts were likewise marked by sincerity. His tears shed at the tomb of Lazarus drew forth even from His enemies the testimony of His sincerity: "Behold how He loved him,"[89] they cried.

His constant rebuke of the insincerity of the Pharisees is the clearest revelation of His own sincere Heart. No one ever stigmatized in stronger or more striking language the vice of insincerity. We almost fear to quote the simple, straightforward words and the strong pictures of which He made use. Vipers, soiled dishes, sepulchers of bones,[90] and other such terms which Christ applied to the hypocrisy and insincerity of the Pharisees are evidence of what Christ thought of the insincere heart and proof of His own pure, crystal sincerity. Insincerity was so loathsome in His sight that His imagination went to the basest, most disgusting pictures of human physical corruption to get language to describe the grossness of the insincere heart.

---

[86] Cf. Ps. 39:8-9 (RSV = Ps. 40:7).
[87] Matt. 26:42.
[88] Cf. John 7:46.
[89] John 11:36.
[90] Matt. 12:34; 23:26, 27.

How to Love as Jesus Loves

Our Lord is often pictured with His Heart revealed to our gaze, and that unveiled prominence has its lesson of sincerity, which may be made clear with the help of a simple English phrase: to wear one's heart on one's sleeve. To wear the heart on the sleeve is to have no secrets from the world, to be transparent to all observers, to have one's thoughts and wishes known even before they find expression upon the lips. The one who wears his heart on his sleeve might desire to be insincere, but could hardly be so in act.

The phrase is not always complimentary in English. It is often used to describe a sudden, effusive, and trustful simplicity which passes for weakness in the opinion of men. The words do not, then, express a quality which most people would care to possess, at least all the time.

But there are occasions when all would perhaps like to wear their hearts on their sleeves: in the worry of a misunderstanding, when our hearts are right but our thoughts are perplexed and explanations seem only to add further complications; in the bitterness of sorrow, when the pressure would be eased and the poison pass away if all could be told as we feel it; and, most of all, in troubles of the conscience, where shame or ignorance of the right terms make us halt and stumble as we try to tell our story. In all these cases, it would be as great a gain to wear our heart on our sleeve as it would be to have the doctor be able to know our most embarrassing diseases without the shameful necessity of telling him. In such cases, we would be glad to reveal ourselves in sincerity as well as in simplicity.

If any such occasion ever arises in our life, we can turn to the Heart of Christ, which He graciously deigns to wear upon His breast so that, with the proofs and tests of His love evident in our eyes, we may be attracted to Him who has no secrets from us and is pleased when we have no secrets from Him. Misunderstanding, sorrow, and troubles of conscience will find relief in our recourse to the Heart of Christ.

He has demanded of us the humility of acknowledging our sins to His priests. His Heart, beating before our eyes in the full attractiveness of this humble, sacrificing love, will draw us to put our confidence in Him, and with the strength of the sincere revelation of His Heart, we will have courage to reveal our sins according to the duty which His merciful justice has laid upon us. The Heart of Christ is not far from us. He has brought it as near to us as He could. Christ stands before us with His Heart fully exposed. That revelation invites our revelation. There is nothing between His heart and ours; there should be nothing between our hearts and His. His sincere Heart should be the forceful incentive to make our hearts sincere to Him and to His ministers.

Finally, Christ gives us the supreme revelation of a sincere heart. "This people honor me with their lips but their hearts are far from me." The distance between the lips and the heart is the measure of sincerity. The nearer those two points are, the greater will be the sincerity. Christ brought the two points together; He identified them. "Having loved His own who were in the world, He loved them to the end."[91] What was the end? Not His death merely. Even beyond that, He gave testimony of His love; beyond that, His Heart spoke. Under the pressure of the centurion's spear, His Heart took lips — lips that spoke of the greatest love man ever had. There is the

[91] John 13:1.

divine model of sincerity, of the heart's voice. There lips and heart are one and identical. The Heart of Christ is the sincere heart, speaking truthfully through the red, rent lips of the true love within.

Chapter Thirteen

∾

Christ gives His Heart
unselfishly to you

"The multitude of believers
had but one heart."

Acts 4:32

∞

That two hearts should beat as one is the ideal, it would seem, of human affection. Such heart duets are scarce enough outside of poetry and fiction. In everyday life, discord arises after only a few beats, and the choir breaks up at the end of the first song.

Heaven's ideal of harmony is something still higher: there are not two or more hearts beating as one; there is only one heart doing the beating for a multitude. There can be no discord; there is only one voice. "And the multitude of believers had but one heart and one soul." There were many veins and arteries, but there was only one heart — a great, warm heart pumping lifeblood through the innumerable ways, reddening, heating, enriching, and invigorating innumerable bodies. One sun is the color and warmth and life of the human race; one heart gives color and warmth and life to Christ's Church.

"The multitude had but one heart." That is, we believe, the greatest miracle of the New Testament; that is convincing proof of the divinity of the Christian Church. God alone could accomplish that tremendous achievement. "And when they had prayed, the place was moved wherein they had assembled; and they were all filled with the Holy Spirit."[92] It was

[92] Acts 4:31.

the Holy Spirit who took the multitude of hearts, melted them in the furnace of Heaven, and then molded one heart for all out of them all.

All unity in some way begins with individual sacrifice and is perfected by one principle. A multitude of sheep become one flock because they acknowledge one shepherd and hearken to one voice that they know. Every sheep has to give up its own inclinations and submit to the inclination of the shepherd. As long as each retains its own voice, they are just sheep; when they take one voice, they become a flock.

What was the sacrifice, what was the unifying principle, that put one great heart into the multitude, that wedded — or rather, that welded — multiplicity into unity? The answer is found in these words: "Neither did anyone say that any of the things which he possessed was his own, but all things were common to them."[93] The sacrifice each one made was of "his own," and the unifying principle was "common to all." Detachment and unselfishness are the instruments that in the hands of the Holy Spirit made the one heart.

The fleshy wrapping of the human heart is called the pericardium and is made of tough sinew. It is painful to stretch it. But the moral pericardium, the selfish wrapping around the human will is tougher still. The early Christians did not try to stretch it; they threw it away, and the Holy Spirit put all their wills inside one large pericardium. They gave up all personal, possessive pronouns of the singular number. "Mine, thine, his," and the like make little hearts; "ours," or rather "God's," makes the great, unselfish, single heart.

[93] Cf. Acts 4:32.

Christ gives His Heart unselfishly

∞

What heart is more unselfish than Christ's Heart? Even the hearts of the early Christians were once selfish, narrow, small, and had to be enlarged; Christ's Heart was made large from the beginning. It was made to hold God's love for men; it was made to hold all men. It was a great miracle indeed to identify the varied wishes of the multitude and bring them by detachment and unselfishness to unite in one wish. It was a marvel to thrill all with the same common love and turn all hearts one way as obediently as all the compasses of the world face one direction under the spell of a magnetic current.

But Christ's detachment and His unselfishness are a divine wonder. Christ could not detach Himself from His divinity. That was Himself. But to all outward appearances, He had done so. The prophets saw Him detached almost from His humanity: "He was a worm, and no man."[94] St. Paul saw Him detached from His royalty: "He emptied Himself, taking the form of a servant."[95] Something harder and more generous in our way of thinking was the detachment of Christ from His own will. His Heart, in the truest sense of the word, was not His own; it was the Father's and ours. Christ sacrificed for us the personal, possessive pronouns: "Not mine,"[96] "the business of the Father,"[97] "the will of the Father,"[98] "the will of Him who

---

[94] Ps. 21:7 (RSV = Ps. 22:6).

[95] Phil. 2:7.

[96] Cf. Luke 22:42.

[97] Cf. Luke 2:49.

[98] Cf. Matt. 7:21.

sent me."[99] This is the language of Christ's Heart, the evidence of the complete identification of His will with the Father's will.

The possessions of the early Christians were anybody's because they were everybody's. Such, too, was the complete surrender of the Heart of Christ to us. Its love is for all and yet as fully for each of us as if each were all. "He loved me; He delivered Himself up for me,"[100] cries St. Paul, and everyone may say the same with similar sublime egotism. There is not a single drop of blood in Christ's Heart that had any other purpose in coming into life, in continuing in life, and going out of life than that. Every drop says, "I love you, I deliver myself up for you, and if you were the only one in existence, my Heart's blood would go out for you." Christ's Heart is the truly unselfish heart that holds the universe and loves all without ceasing to love each.

How eager that unselfish Heart was to show that its contents had but one purpose: to be shed for us! Christ's blood was deeply stirred in the garden of Gethsemane at the spectacle of the Passion. It felt straitened until that great work should be accomplished. If the casing of His Heart tried to restrain that bubbling flood, then, in its supreme unselfishness, it would know what to do: as in Gethsemane, it would break through the barriers of flesh and form beads and streams of ruddy sweat, anticipating in unselfish eagerness the Calvary of the morrow.[101]

[99] John 4:34.
[100] Gal. 2:20.
[101] Luke 22:44.

Chapter Fourteen

∽

Christ enlightens your heart

"He was grieved for the blindness
of their hearts."

Mark 3:5

∞

"Blindness of heart" is a strange phrase. The heart feels, worries, and loves, but does the heart see? And how can the heart be blind?

For us, the heart more commonly means the source of willing and feeling, less commonly the source of thinking. But in Scripture, the heart often means the mind, yet always with a shade of difference. When the mind thinks, the truth may be bright and clear, but it is cold, like sunlight in the arctic zone; when the heart thinks, the truth is warm, like sunlight in warmer zones. The will is never far away when there is talk about the heart, and when our Blessed Lady was pondering the words and deeds of her Son in her heart,[102] it was, we may be sure, no idle reverie, but a deliberate act of the warmest love that made her think and kept her thinking. Knowledge precedes love, and love precedes knowledge. We will to open our eyes, and we see to will some more.

"Blindness of heart" is a strange phrase, but it is a serious one and implies a state that filled the gentle Lord with grief and anger. Witness the vivid picture given to us by St. Mark when, on the Sabbath, Christ healed a man with the withered hand: "And looking round about on them with anger, being

[102]Cf. Luke 2:19.

107

grieved for the blindness of their hearts . . . "[103] There was a lightning flash of anger in the glance which swept the circle of Pharisees on that eventful Sabbath, and that flash, or the look of sad pity which succeeded it, should have found its way through the blindness of even a pharisaical heart. There was something of the same vexation, although tempered with more grief, when our Lord had to reproach His Apostles for blindness of heart: "Do you not yet know or understand? Have you still your heart blinded?"[104] The Pharisees were blind because they would not see, but the Apostles were blind because they *could* not see.

There is a blindness of heart which closes its eyes to all light. Of such blindness there is scarcely question in the texts cited. There is, however, another blindness which falsifies the light — color blindness — and another still which dims the light, a kind of shortsightedness.

The Pharisees saw something. They saw the law. But like people whose eyes do not respond to certain colors, they were blind to the spirit and purpose of the law. The law is not an end in itself. It is made for a purpose, it exists for a purpose, and willfully to close one's eyes to that purpose is to be blind of heart.

Christ gave the Pharisees enough light. He taught them by statement of the spirit of the Sabbath law, but all this was wasted on the Pharisees. Christ cured the withered hand before their eyes and put His teaching into the terse balance of an epigram: "The Sabbath was made for man, and not man for

---

[103] Mark 3:5.
[104] Mark 8:17.

the Sabbath."[105] All in vain! The Pharisees, "going out imme-diately, made a consultation how they might destroy Him."[106]

What is this terrible blindness which can resist so much light? It is pride of will. No one is so blind as he who will not see. To admit that Christ was right was to confess that they were wrong, to submit to His teaching, to obey His decisions, and to make an open acknowledgment to their own little world that they were inferior to their new teacher. His words were clear and His proofs were convincing, but their wills were proud and stubborn. They did not simply cover their eyes or close them with lids which might readily part again. Rather, they blinded themselves, refusing to yield free obedi-ence to the teaching of Christ. The Pharisees plucked out the eye of their heart and would not see Christ's interpretation of the law.

The Apostles were blind as well, but their blindness was due to a lack of light, not to a rejection of the light. Their vi-sion had not been destroyed. It needed, however, to be recti-fied. When Christ told them to beware of the leaven of the Pharisees, the Apostles understood Him literally, and they were somewhat alarmed, because most of their bakers be-longed to the Pharisees. There was to be no more bread for them, they thought. Christ had to tell them that the leaven of the Pharisees meant the Pharisees' hypocrisy, their evil doc-trines, which would secretly permeate and corrupt the soul. He reminded His Apostles that He had fed thousands with only a few loaves and fish, and there were baskets of fragments

[105]Mark 2:27.
[106]Mark 3:6.

left over.[107] But He talked to men whose spiritual eyesight was dim, whose souls were not lifted above the tangible and sensible, whose vision was hampered by the material and did not pierce to the spiritual. "Have you still your heart blinded?"

Blind of heart are those whose whole lives are given to pleasures and to the gratification of the senses. Blind of heart are those who make wealth the only good and the supreme good. Blind of heart are those to whom applause is the sweetest of sounds, and a high position the greatest delight. All these do not savor the things of God. To speak to them of the delights of prayer, of the consolation of Communion, or of peace of conscience is to use a foreign language. They hear the words and note the gestures, but they cannot fathom the meaning. A man of no literary tastes cannot understand the enjoyment of poetry. A man of blinded heart looks on religion and its practices as so many mysteries. He cannot imagine that they possess any charm, and he deems religious people weakminded or unbalanced.

∽

The so-called nebular theory is a possible explanation of the universe; it may be true or further explanations may prove it false, but it will serve to illustrate solidly established fact.

The Incarnation witnessed the creation of another light: the light of the moral world. God had said, "Let there be light, and light was made."[108] In the Incarnation, He may be considered to have said, "Let there be love, and the Heart of Christ

---

[107]Cf. Mark 8:15-20.
[108]Gen. 1:3.

was made." If the primitive nebula, which theory conjectures, contained all the energy of the universe, the Heart of Christ, which was God's love made flesh, is the burning source of all light, heat, and motion in the universe of souls. Into that Heart was poured the ocean of God's love, and out of it has flowed every drop of grace which has exercised an effect in this world.

"Of His fullness we all have received."[109] Out of the reservoir of His love, which God created for us at the Incarnation and opened for us upon the Cross came the universe of grace, with its planets and suns and moons and constellations, which light up and adorn the firmament of the new creation. This firmament is more brilliant than the firmament which God's omnipotence arched over our head when He said, "Let there be light," and broader, because this arch stretches its span far into a horizonless eternity. From the brief splendor of the passing thought or wish which prompts to repentance or lights the way to higher virtue, to the undimmed and steady radiance of the holiest soul's highest sanctity, all light came from the fire kindled by the Heart of Christ.

Apostles and missionaries carry that light into the darkness of paganism. The Church's Doctors and teachers use it to explore the innermost recesses of baffling truths. The pastors of the Church, from priest to Pope, have the guidance of the Light of the World when they lead their flocks along the ways which pass from night to eternal day. Christ is the light which enlightens every man who comes into the world,[110] and the Heart of Christ is the center and source of that tremendous

[109] John 1:16.
[110] Cf. John 1:9.

and unfailing energy. The light of the world was kindled into flame by the love of His Heart.

In the narrower world of the blinded individual, the Heart of Christ is the light, the healer of blindness. Christ became a victim to laws blindly interpreted. His Heart was laid open in obedience to law. The spear that pierced His side on the Cross is the fit instrument and fit emblem of law blindly interpreted. A blind law is cold, edged with sharpness, and relentless. So was that spear. Like the spear, pride may be broken, but it refuses to bend.

But God's law came in obedience, in humility, in love; it came in a heart. Whenever love goes with the law, there will be no blindness to the spirit of the law. When Christ's Heart was opened on the Cross, all blind hearts won the power to open their closed eyes to the light and to see the light, just as Longinus,[111] the centurion, saw the light, threw away his rigid spear, and became a saint.

The loving heart will not be blind to the purpose of the law and will rightly interpret the meaning of the law. Love will cure color blindness and shortsightedness. The heart never forgets the person for whose benefit the law is, for the law is not for the pride of the ruler but for the good of the ruled. The heart does not miss the meaning of the law. The eyes of charity see all and see deep.

When the hearts of the Apostles had been formed by living with Christ, by seeing Him die, by feeling His love and

---

[111]Longinus is the name traditionally given to the soldier who pierced Christ's side with his spear. According to legend, he became a Christian and died a martyr.

learning to love Him in return — when, in a word, their hearts were made like His Heart — no longer did they misinterpret His meaning. With the instinct of love, they went to the meaning of Christ's words. Some hidden selfishness, perhaps the urgent thought of their bodily necessities, made the Apostles' hearts blind when they heard their teacher speak of the leaven of the Pharisees. There was only one kind of a yeast for them. But when love ruled supreme, they went to the heart of things. They understood and were shortsighted no more.

To cure blindness perfectly, there is need of two things: good light and good sight. The Heart of Christ furnishes both remedies in full perfection for blindness of heart. It was His Heart, love incarnate, that became the light of the world. It was His Heart that gave good eyes to the hearts of men by showing them that love must enforce the law and interpret the law. By dying under the spear of tyranny and ignorance, the Heart of Christ won the grace for all to see, and it became the medium for all to see, the crystal lens of love rectifying the imperfect visions of men.

Chapter Fifteen

∞

You will find sympathy in Christ's Heart

"The heart of this people
is grown gross."

Matthew 13:15

∞

Sympathy is the nurse for illness of the soul. It smiles with hope when one is despondent. It is gentle and soothing when one is in anguish. And when the final crisis comes, and the soul hovers between life and death, sympathy never leaves the side of the sufferer; it eases the pain by every possible means and tempers the fever when it ranges alarmingly above normal. How sensitive sympathy is and how swift! When the thoughts race — and thought is faster than light — sympathy outstrips them all. Sympathy even anticipates the slow mind. It is prophetic; it foresees.

If sympathy is swifter than thought, its home must be in the heart, and not in the mind, and so it is. Surely charity is of the heart, and sympathy is nothing more than winged charity. Anything that will weigh down the heart will clip the wings of sympathy and fetter its flight.

Our Lord and His Apostles looked for sympathy and, we have sad reason to believe, often lacked it. Thus, they often quoted this passage from Isaiah: "And the prophecy of Isaiah is fulfilled in them, who saith, 'By hearing, you shall hear and shall not understand, and seeing, you shall see and shall not perceive. For the heart of this people is grown gross.' "[112]

[112] Cf. Matt. 13:14-15.

The heart that is gross (the word means fat, dull, heavy) is not sympathetic. It stops sympathy at the fountainhead. Instead of being sensitive, it is callous; instead of being prophetic, it is blind and deaf. Such a heart cannot fly; it cannot crawl; it is tied to itself and caged within the narrow limits of selfishness. The great English dramatist William Shakespeare has said the final word on the last stage of the gross heart, lost to all sense and feeling. He describes a heart in which there has not been merely degeneration by the deposit of fat in the muscles of the heart, but the complete absorption of the heart in fat. "Duller shouldst thou be," says the ghost of his father to Hamlet, "than the fat weed that roots itself in ease on Lethe wharf."[113]

Not a single element of that picture should be lost, not "weed," nor "roots," nor "ease," nor "Lethe" — the land of complete forgetfulness — nor "wharf," where the well-watered weeds grow rankest, if one would get a complete view of the gross heart which Isaiah complained of when he was entering upon his mission, and the gross heart our Lord and His Apostles found in the audiences to whom they appealed. They looked for sympathetic hearts, but, in many cases, found gross hearts that closed eye and ear and every avenue of knowledge to the message of Christ, hearts that would not let even a whisper of Christ's voice stir their weedy fibers as they slumbered in forgetfulness and ease forevermore.

∾

To have a sympathetic heart of the truest kind, there are three requisites: unselfishness, knowledge, and experience. As

[113]*Hamlet*, Act 1, scene 5.

the magnet looks northward, so sympathy looks outward. Sympathy is essentially unselfish; it is the flower of Christian civilization.

Besides unselfishness, sympathy calls for knowledge. We must know another's sorrow and pain in order to feel for him. But knowledge is not enough for perfect sympathy: experience, which, after all, is the ripest knowledge, produces the truest sympathy. The one who can say, "I have suffered in the same way myself " is likely to have the most sympathetic heart.

Now, where can these three elements be found in greater completeness than in the Heart of Christ? That Heart was utterly unselfish. It was made for others. It was a gift to us. It came into existence like a letter addressed to us. A letter is not at all for itself; it is for the one to whom it is addressed. The Heart of Christ has the same unselfishness and its contents are wholly for us. Each drop of its blood is for us, as well as all the gathered drops in the precious receptacle of His Heart.

Not a single soul of all mankind was excluded from His sympathy. "God so loved the world as to give . . . "[114] The gift to the world was to all. Christ does not withhold the blood of His Heart from anyone. It goes to everyone. If it does not reach its destination, it is because the human will rejects the gift. In our sympathy, we transmit feeling by means of words; in Christ's sympathy, His Heart brings its healing blood to His suffering ones by means of His infinite power everywhere present.

Christ was able to read the hearts of men. "He knew their thoughts; He knew what was in man"[115] — such statements

[114]John 3:16.
[115]Luke 6:8; John 2:25.

occur frequently in the Gospel. As God, He had the unique privilege of being the searcher of hearts. The Heart of Christ could therefore be sympathetic. As for experience of pain and sorrow, who that has read Isaiah's prophecy and its more than perfect fulfillment in the Passion can mention a kind of pain or grief, or a degree of pain and grief, which Christ did not experience in His life and death? Theologians have weighed and numbered His sorrows: saints have, with the ingenuity of love, described and valued them.

For all of us, there is proof that we can see and hear. Our eyes are fascinated with the horror of His bloody sweat which reveals in lurid red how His blood fled in terror from the prospects of anguish and torment.[116] Our ears are chilled with the cry of divine abandonment which springs out of the soul of Christ from the consummation of His torture: "My God, my God, why hast thou forsaken me?"[117]

The Heart of Christ must have been sympathetic, and a reading of His life story shows that it was. Sympathy is the promptness of charity, the delicate refinement of the rarest love. To show all that in Christ's Heart is simply to rehearse the Gospel.

Take an instance which no one can fail to understand. Children are most susceptible to sympathy. They do not reason about it; they feel it. The pretense of it can scarcely escape their detection. Then remember how the children flocked around Christ and felt at home near His Heart, whereas the well-meaning Apostles felt, we may imagine, as awkward as a

[116]Luke 22:44.
[117]Matt. 27:46.

locomotive colliding with the fragile lace of a spider's gossamer web.[118]

Christ's dealing with sinners is another luminous revelation of His sympathetic Heart. The world of His day could not understand it. If they could avoid it, the self-righteous of His day would not even tread upon the same earth as sinners. Christ's Heart had no such unsympathetic aloofness. In Christ's presence, proud, sensitive sinners who hardened into stone under the scorn of the world melted into tears of repenting sorrow.

Let us rest the proof of the sympathy of the Heart of Christ on the conduct of the mothers who brought their children to Christ, on the actions of Mary Magdalene,[119] and on the tears of Peter, who succumbed to one glance of sympathy.[120]

[118]Cf. Matt. 19:13.
[119]Cf. Matt. 26:7.
[120]Luke 22:61-62.

Chapter Sixteen

∞

Christ understands your own hurts and calls you to forgive others

"So also shall my heavenly Father do to you, if you forgive not your brother from your hearts."

Matthew 18:35

∞

Great criminals sometimes achieve a certain distinction denied to the starving pauper who takes a loaf of bread. Such is the case of the servant in the Gospel who was forgiven a debt of millions of dollars. No one could be proud of so gigantic a deficit in his account, and it should scarcely astonish us that the possessor of this distinction throttled a fellow servant whose deficit was just a few dollars, a million times less than his own. Unhappily for the criminal, the master of both servants did not consider the size of the debts a significant factor, and, revoking the gift of millions which he had made by canceling a lawful debt, he delivered the greater debtor to the torture until he should pay all. The amount of that torture is appalling, but more appalling are the words with which the story concludes: "So also shall my heavenly Father do to you, if you forgive not your brother from your hearts."[121]

No doubt our Lord purposely made this parable striking in its details — details which could be the case only where God is the master who forgives infinite offenses and men are the slaves who do not forgive petty faults. In reality, however, it is almost unbelievable that any master would let his servant accumulate so immense a debt, and almost impossible that any

[121]Matt. 18:23-35.

man would be so mean, so contemptible, so small of heart as to turn around and throttle his fellow when he had so much forgiven himself. We say "almost impossible," because man's selfishness is so colossal and his imagination can so exaggerate his own troubles and so minimize his neighbor's troubles that no inconsistency of conduct is astonishing where wounded self-love and a heated fancy brood on wrongs.

One great reason why forgiveness from the heart is so scarce among men is to be found in the exaggerations of self-love. We think that no one deserves the consideration to which we are entitled. Our wrongs are so great, so personal, so intimate to us that no one else, we think, can appreciate them at their true value. We can always see reasons why others should feel their wrongs less keenly, but in our case, there is something about the person or the time or the manner of the injury that persuades our brooding and distempered minds that we have discovered a new, unheard of species of sorrow — ours.

No doubt the servant in the Gospel was a victim of such stupendous self-love. Like a watchmaker, he placed a magnifying glass over one eye and turned its gaze upon the tiny little sum owed to him until it assumed gigantic proportions, and tightly closed his other eye, which ought to have been looking at what he owed his master. He exaggerated others' debts; he obliterated his own.

It is a calumny upon the honorable profession of watchmakers to liken them to unforgiving hearts. The watchmaker, at any rate, has this consolation: his work is useful and necessary, and when he has finished it, his face, which is contorted in concentration during his work, resumes its accustomed grace and beauty. But the unlovely, strained looks of an unforgiving heart never relax into peace and sweetness. Equipped with magnifying glass on one eye and an impenetrable blinder on the other, the unforgiving heart shuts out the whole world and brings its bent, peering gaze to bear upon the lifelong contemplation and distortion of its wrongs.

∞

Forgiveness of enemies was a virtue dear to the Heart of Christ. It is one of those virtues, like humility and virginity, which are so sublime and so opposed to the natural impulses of human nature that their revelation and teaching by Christ seems to many to prove His divinity. Surely, then, if He may be said to love one virtue more than another, it would be one which was His own because He was the first to teach it to the world.

His revelation of this virtue was as perfect as it was new, and in that, we may see another reason why the forgiveness of enemies was dear to His Heart. No one has conceived or can conceive a single perfection which may be added to this virtue taught by Christ. Forgiveness, as Christ teaches, should be perfect in extent, including all; perfect in its promptness, not letting the sun go down upon its anger; and perfect in its practice, not calling another a fool, not exacting an eye for an eye, not harboring evil thoughts or judging him.[122] So thought, word, and deed were to be filled with forgiveness.

The virtue was no less perfect in its continuous performance. The forgiving of trespassers was to be as regular as the petition for daily bread. There was to be no limit to the number

[122]Cf. Eph. 4:26; Matt. 5:22, 38-40, 9:4, 7:1.

of times it was to be exercised. Its exercise, if necessary, would reach the perfect number: "seventy times seven times."[123] Forgiveness was to be the perfect badge of Christ's followers: "By this, all men shall know you."[124]

It was to be perfect in its sincerity, forgiving from the heart; perfect in its sanction, because in what measure we mete to others, it shall be meted to us; and, finally, perfect in its model and standard, because we are to forgive as Christ forgave: we are to be merciful as our heavenly Father is merciful.

Forgiveness is difficult because self enters so fully into the wrongs and because the wrongs have been so exaggerated by the imagination. The Heart of Christ, by meeting and overcoming these two difficulties, is the model of the forgiving heart and the healing of all unforgiving hearts. The unforgiving heart is selfish, but the Heart of Christ is entirely unselfish. The unforgiving heart exaggerates the faults done to it, but the Heart of Christ has endured wrongs and sees in them a malice which, because it is infinite, cannot be exaggerated.

In the depths of eternity, what was God's view of the Heart of Christ? Some answer that He saw it as a vessel full of the fire of love; others — and they are more numerous — declare that the Heart of Christ never appeared in the thoughts of God as anything other than a suffering, wounded Heart, created to be crucified, to be pierced, and to die. Christ's Heart was made to be a holocaust for sin. From first to last, and in every part of its brimming contents, it was destined for others and for the sins of others. It was to be the great peacemaker

---

[123]Matt. 18:21.
[124]John 13:35.

between infinite worth and infinite offense, between God and God's enemy.

The Heart of Christ, then, had not a trace of the taint of unforgiveness. It was planned from eternity for forgiveness; it was created in time for forgiveness; it lived and died for the same divine purpose. The Heart of Christ is forgiveness itself. It is mercy in its most winning and most perfect form — mercy made into a Heart.

How well, then, the Heart of Christ serves as a model of the forgiving heart! No selfishness there; no acute sensitiveness to receive and retain wrongs. It was pure unselfishness, utterly flawless forgiveness.

A diamond is transfigured carbon, changed from density and darkness into marvelous brilliance by the power of crystallization. Imagine all the carbon of the world collected into one mass, heated to glowing incandescence, subjected to the necessary pressure, and allowed to cool so that every atom would fall into line in obedience to the marshaling forces of crystallization. Then you would have a diamond planet without a flaw or blemish, which would flash back the garnered sheaves of sunlight in blinding splendor.

A poet's dream you say. Yet the Heart of Christ is more wonderful still. Infinite love has transfigured it into total unselfishness. It gathers up into itself God's infinite mercy, and pours it back upon the enemies of God, making every drop of His blood to reflect God's infinite forgiveness.

The unforgiving heart is not only selfish, but it exaggerates its wrongs. Humorists are fond of showing how a lively imagination and a poor nervous condition can bring upon a man more diseases in an hour than he could get in the contagious ward of a hospital in a century. Wrongs and offended dignity are, if possible, worse victims of the tyrant imagination than weak nerves are. Does the Heart of our Lord meet this weakness of the unforgiving heart? It does, and most successfully.

Let us take, unforgiving heart, the very wrong which infuriates you most, which has been turned into a monster by a heated imagination. The Heart of Christ felt that very same wrong, has seen in it not any false malice manufactured by temporary madness, but the true malice of it, which far exceeds the powers of imagination. His Heart is more tender than yours and has felt your wrong more keenly than you have, and has felt it longer than you have, because He felt it from His first heartbeat to His last. You are wounded for one reason: because you are offended. Christ is wounded for two reasons: because He is offended and because you are. He feels your wrong, because His is your brother, because your wrong is His wrong, and because your wrong is God's wrong.

There is, then, a malice in your wrong which Christ knows and feels in His Heart — a malice that is infinite. You think it is a great thing that you should be offended; our Lord understands that it is an infinitely greater thing that God should be offended. The Heart of Christ, therefore, says to you, unforgiving heart, "I have understood your wrong better than you, have seen it so black that it could not be blacker, have felt it more deeply because it was more mine than yours, have forgiven it after all, and have died for it." What will you answer to that appeal, unforgiving heart?

And yet that is not all the Heart of Christ has done. It has not only forgiven the wrongs done to it, but also, by a divine refinement of mercy and charity, it changed the blow it was dealt into a benefit for the hand that dealt the blow. The Heart of Christ conferred on its murderers the power of salvation and life everlasting by the very act in which they robbed it of life, dying for those who were killing it, saving those who were slaying it. The blood that rushed from the Heart of Christ went speeding upon an errand of mercy, hurrying out to heal its enemies and destroyers with warm, eternal, infinite forgiveness.

Chapter Seventeen

Christ's Heart teaches you to love God above all

"The Devil now put it into
the heart of Judas Iscariot
to betray Him."

John 13:2

∞

An Irish orator was very fond of trees. Near his house there was a very fine one, whose growth he watched with care and whose beauty he grew to love. As the years went on, the tree grew and spread and finally encroached upon his house, blocking the light and pushing here and there against the walls and roof with its branches, seeking a chance to expand. "You will have to cut down that tree," said his friend. "I was thinking of taking down the house," replied the orator.

The human heart has its growths, which it loves and watches and makes sacrifices to, and to deal with that tendency we have the virtue of detachment. Detachment plants in the proper place, keeps rank growth well pruned, and, if need be, lays the axe to the root rather than lose a greater good. It saves the house rather than the tree. To the orator, the tree may have been more valuable than the house, but to detachment, the soul is more valuable than its attachments. Detachment is at the head of the bureau for the conservation of spiritual resources. It does not permit the energies of the soul to be wasted or monopolized by passion to the exclusion of the soul's supreme interest: God Himself. Detachment, then, uproots or controls all attachments except one: attachment to God.

The Gospel gives the complete history of a disastrous attachment which grew, overshadowed the soul, and finally destroyed the soul. St. John tells us the last stage: "The Devil now put it into the heart of Judas Iscariot to betray Him." Detachment said, "You will have to give up that attachment to the purse." "I will give up Christ," replied Judas. The Devil had easy access into that attached heart.

The attachment of Judas did not grow in a day. To leave all and follow Christ shows no roots of avarice in the heart, but at least the seeds of the highest holiness. Judas left all, yet, with the weak inconsistency of human nature, he let the strings of a purse wind about his heart, as Peter, with like weakness and inconsistency, was willing to face, and no doubt would have faced, a thousand sword blades, but was cowed by the accusing tongue of one maid.[125]

Judas alone could tell us how attraction changed to inclination, how inclination blossomed into evil desire, and how evil desire branched out into the full growth of attachment. Then came the blocking out of the light, the overshadowing of dark principles, and the unchecked wild struggle for mastery. This was the stage of deceit when attachment decked itself out as a virtue.

"Why was not this ointment sold for three hundred pieces of silver and given to the poor?"[126] asked Judas when Mary anointed the feet of Jesus, and from the Gospel it seems that he whispered this hypocrisy to the other Apostles. They were deceived and, in good but mistaken faith, took up the complaint. There you have a picture of the essential meanness of attachment. It would not be too much to believe that Judas

[125]Cf. Luke 22:33, 56-57.
[126]John 12:5.

kept in the background, while his poisoned dupes fought his battles for him. Cowardice, meanness, hypocrisy, poisoning of souls: such are the deadly fruits of attachment.

The final stage came when attachment was fully grown. It staggers us to think that a man would sell another man for thirty pieces of silver. That was the price to be paid for a murdered slave.[127] Judas accepted the pittance with its insulting connotations and agreed to betray Jesus. It was money or Christ; and attachment, with its blinding, grappling hold upon his soul, had its way, and Christ was crucified.

No doubt other motives helped avarice at the end, but a full-grown attachment so exaggerates the object of its selfishness as to debase and pervert every other noble instinct of the soul. The shock of the completed crime alone opens the eyes again, and then God's infinite mercy must be grasped and clung to, or the heinous foulness of the attachment's cancerous growth will excite the loathing of despair.

The successive stages of attachment are: love of earthly good for God and with God, love of earthly good and God, love of earthly good without God, and love of earthly good against God. The Heart of Christ, which belonged to God, the Second Person of the Blessed Trinity, could never pass out of the first stage. It was and ever will be for God and with God. It does, however, give us a picture of perfect detachment, meeting and counteracting the various stages of attachment: the planting, the overshadowing, and the final struggle.

[127] Cf. Exod. 21:32.

When Christ our Lord looked into the world to choose a mother and a place of birth and a manner of life, all the attractions of earth lay before Him: wealth, honor, intellect, power, comfort, and pleasure. He passed them all by and chose Mary, Bethlehem, and Calvary — purity, poverty, and pain. So the seed of every human attachment was banished at once from the Heart of Christ, and therein was planted the love of virtue, holiness, and suffering. When Christ picked out a Heart for Himself, He took one that was wounded and girt with thorns. Attachment loves the velvet touch of pleasure and the crown of gold and cannot grow beneath the painful points of the thorns and the spear.

Christ also manifested to us His detachment in opposing the second stage of attachment, where vice masquerades as virtue, and when selfishness is substituted in the soul for God. It was in the desert that Christ allowed Satan to tempt Him and thus reveal to us His Heart, turning to naught the vain deceits of the evil one.[128] It was not to open sensuality that Christ was tempted. Although the Devil's temptation of Christ to turn stones into bread was opportunely timed, coming after Christ's long fast, it was subtly cloaked under the exercise of power. It offered a chance for Him to indulge in deception, to seek the gratification of the flesh under the guise of doing good. Christ unmasked the tempter. No attachment to bread alone will give the soul life.

Again, it was not to open pride of life that Christ was tempted in the second instance, when the Devil tempted Christ to hurl Himself from the Temple, saying that angels

---

[128]Matt. 14:1-11; Mark 1:13; Luke 4:2-13.

would prevent His fall. This pride was deceitfully allied with the Temple, God's angels, and God's Providence, circumstances that seemed to justify an exhibition of power on His part. But Christ was not to assert His power in the Temple, nor was God to be thus tempted.

Finally, the evil one promised to crown Him king of the world, when he offered Christ all kingdoms in return for worshiping him. Attachment enthrones the same king, and attachment uses the same means that the tempter used for Christ. Imaginary pleasures, imaginary power and glory, are spread before the bewitched eyes of the mind. Dreams of new worlds of delight, brittle and brilliant, are the deceitful creations of attachment. Christ bursts the bubble. Not self, but the Lord God alone is to be adored and served.

Christ is also our example and our stay in the final struggle against attachment in the death grapple between soul and selfishness. In the hour of His agony in the garden, there were many sorrows that came to lay their burden upon the stricken Savior, but of the presence of one heavy sorrow we may be sure. In His agony, Christ struggled with the attachment of all attachments: the love of life. He saw, He felt His enemies, not simply severing one desire from His Heart, but laying the axe of torture and death to the very juncture of heart and life. If ever the axe was laid to the root of attachment, it was in that hour. All the attachments of man come from and go back to one great attachment: the love of self. Self will let the soul be lost rather than lose its own gratification. What, then, will self feel when not one or another pleasure is threatened but its own existence is in doubt? The love of life is more than the love of pleasure or power.

How to Love as Jesus Loves

"Not my will, but Thine be done!" The detached Heart of Christ makes the supreme sacrifice. It slays self, immolates attachment to life, and offers the holocaust to God. God is never overshadowed or crowded out in the detached heart, and Christ had the most detached of all hearts beating in His breast.

Chapter Eighteen

∞

Christ's Heart embraces all

"Thou shalt love the Lord, thy God,
with thy whole heart."

Matthew 22:37

～

The great horizons of the world make our eyes ache. The level stretches of the heaving ocean, the depths of the heavens when the cold north wind contracts the stars into brilliant points and gives them perspective, the vast length of the sky across which the thunder sounds, and whose chasm the lightning spans in its leap: these daze and bewilder us.

The horizons of the soul are vaster, and never, perhaps, is the spiritual eye more likely to waver and fail than when it strives to pierce the length and width and breadth of the tremendous words of Christ: "Thou shalt love the Lord, thy God, with thy whole heart and with thy whole soul and with thy whole mind." Immense indeed is the scope of this "first and greatest commandment"![129] Sunrise gives us a worldwide horizon; this commandment is a dawn in the moral order, dispelling darkness, clearing up the outlook, and widening the gaze to the infinite depths of the heart, the infinite height of the soul, and the infinite width of the mind.

We are commanded to give our whole heart to God. There are no fractions, no small currency in His mart. We do not give Him so much and wait for the change. He takes all our gold. We are commanded to be wholehearted, not halfhearted, and

[129]Matt. 22:38.

143

it is within our power to be so, for God does not command impossibilities.

It is to be noted what this command means; otherwise our soul will surely be bewildered. "Thou shalt love with thy whole heart." We are bid to love with all the heart that belongs to us, with all the heart that comes within the control of our will. The will does not open or shut at its pleasure the floodgates of tears. It does not light up the eyes with happiness or darken them with sorrow as it wishes. It can spread a smile on the face, but cannot prevent it at times from being no more than muscular. In a word, our feelings are partly rooted in the body, and may be as much beyond our voluntary control as digestion is. The manifestation of feeling may be checked; its presence or absence cannot always be managed as we desire. "With thy whole heart" does not mean with tears or smiles. If we long to have these trimmings of human love, that very longing bathes our heart with tears or wreathes it with laughter, even if our lips are marble and our eyes a sandy desert without an oasis. "With thy whole heart" does not mean feeling, which we cannot always have; the phrase does mean willing, an action we can always do.

We love God with our whole heart when we do not give our service to false gods or to God's enemies, when we rate God at the highest price in the universe, and His infinite excellence makes it possible and reasonable always to do that. We love God with our whole heart when word and thought and act and all our life have but one bent and direction, which is toward Him.

The right love of self, of family, of friends, and of country are not fractions taken from God's love; on the contrary, they are the parts which make up that love. If the stream flows toward God, not one of those currents must be diverted from paying its due tribute to the sea. The mother weeping in wild grief for her dead child is loving God with her whole heart. God gave her a mother's heart; He imparted a share of His infinite loveliness to her lost one, and in her very cry and heartache is made vocal the void which God left in us to be filled by Him. The mother would like to, but perhaps cannot, shower on God, as she does on her child, the flood of her tears or the wealth of her smiles, but while she recognizes in the loveliness of her little one even a tiny drop of God's infinite lovableness, she is wholehearted in her love for her child and for her God.

∞

The Heart of Christ will show us how to weave the separate and various strands of human love into the vesture of many colors, "without a seam,"[130] which is to be placed at the feet of God. It would be a mistake to think that the Heart of Jesus did not thrill with the affections which He has implanted in our hearts and wishes us to manifest according to His law. His teaching reveals His Heart. The touching picture of the mother hen gathering her chickens, which described His love for His people, and the images of the good shepherd, of the woman's search for her lost coin, and of the more than earthly father of the prodigal son,[131] which tell of His love for sinners, put before us clearly and tenderly the affections of Christ's Heart.

[130]John 19:23.
[131]Cf. Matt. 23:37; John 10:11, 14-16; Luke 15:8-9, 11-32.

His friendships are even more significant than His words. They are not all the same. They had an appropriateness in their variety. Mary, His mother, and Mary Magdalene, John and Peter, Lazarus, and Martha all found a place in His Heart, and to each He accorded an individual love, suitable and fitting. The knowledge He had of each was varied; the friendship followed suit.

The manifestation of these friendships was also different. His Heart showed itself in tears at the tomb of Lazarus, flashed forth a melting look for Peter, thrilled in the deepest tenderness when He called Mary Magdalene by name, and was lavished on His mother and St. Joseph through thirty years of loving subjection.[132]

In spite of, or, rather, because of, all these friendships for those whom He met in life — friendships that are repeated in every soul that turns to Him — the friendship of Christ for His Father was wholehearted. Indeed, so vigorously, so sternly did He assert the absolute claims of His Father that shortsighted criticism forgets that Christ knew the fourth commandment,[133] forgets that He was lovingly subject to His mother ten times longer than He worked openly for the world and that she was in His thoughts as He died.[134] Criticism forgets all this because it forgets that the love of the mother can be, and must be, united with the love of God.

The fire of wholeheartedness purifies and converts into its own rising flames all the fuel that it touches. Listen to the

---

[132]Cf. John 11:35; Luke 22:61; John 20:16; Luke 2:51.

[133]"Honor thy mother and father"; cf. Exod. 20:12.

[134]John 19:26-27.

strong language of wholeheartedness: "Whosoever shall do the will of my Father, who is in Heaven, he is my brother and sister and mother."[135] "If any man come to me and hate not his father and mother and wife and children and brethren and sisters, yea, and his own life also, he cannot be my disciple."[136] These are other ways of saying what Christ said in the first commandment: "Thou shalt love the Lord, thy God, *with thy whole heart.*" His life and His Heart show us how these words are to be understood. God must not have any rivals; to Him all must be directed. Whatever feelings may dictate — whether they make willing easy by going with the will or make willing hard by going the other way — the will must, as it can, be wholehearted in preferring God to any created thing when the soul stands at the parting of the ways. It can, and it must, love the friends God gives, but it must stop short at sin. The heart must be wholehearted.

Look at the love of the Heart of Jesus. It was wholehearted in extent for men: "Having loved His own, He loved them unto the end."[137] It was wholehearted in extent for God: "He was obedient to death, even to the death of the Cross."[138] "Unto," "even to," are the badges of wholeheartedness.

The love of Christ was wholehearted in its nature. It went forth to creatures without straying from God. The splendor of the sun may be separated by crystal glass or crystal water into its various component colors; the rainbow hues may again be

[135]Mark 3:35.
[136]Luke 14:26.
[137]John 13:1.
[138]Phil. 2:8.

blended into the whiteness from which they came. The love from the Heart of Christ went forth in all its varied beauty to many hearts on earth, but it did not stay centered and arrested in any one, but, uniting its rays, passed on again to God. God is "the Alpha and the Omega,"[139] the beginning and the end of the whole heart, and the Heart of Christ was the most complete of whole hearts.

[139]Rev. 1:8.

Biographical Note
∞

Francis P. Donnelly, S.J.

(1869-1959)

⚭

Born in Pittston, Pennsylvania, Francis Donnelly inherited a love for reading from his mother, who was a schoolteacher. This passion for reading not only contributed to his success as a writer, poet, and teacher, but also led him to pursue a vocation in the Society of Jesus. As a youth, inspired by the courage of the early Jesuit missionaries in Canada and impressed by the size of the Jesuit Order, which had more members than any other order at the time, he resolved to become a Jesuit priest. While faithfully praying a daily litany to St. Ignatius of Loyola, the founder of the Society of Jesus, he attended the Augustinian college at Villanova and Fordham University before entering the Jesuit novitiate in Maryland, where he was ordained a priest in 1903.

Aside from serving for a year as assistant editor of the Jesuit periodical *The Messenger of the Sacred Heart* and another year as rector of Gonzaga College, in Washington, DC, Fr. Donnelly devoted most of his priesthood to teaching rhetoric at various Jesuit schools. In the classroom and in his articles and educational textbooks, he encouraged his students to learn the fine art of composition in the way he had learned it: from reading.

A gifted poet, Fr. Donnelly wrote the lyrics to hundreds of songs, many of them about Ireland. His literary talent was also manifested in his devotional books, through which he said he preached to himself as well as to others. In moving and consoling words, he reveals his compassionate understanding of the human heart, with its needs and yearnings, which are fulfilled in the Sacred Heart of Jesus, our hearts' model and strength. Guiding his readers through Scripture, Fr. Donnelly leads Christians to a profound realization of Christ's personal love for each and every soul.